Storm
over
Ethics

STORM
OVER
ETHICS

JOHN C. BENNETT
JAMES M. GUSTAFSON
E. CLINTON GARDNER
GABRIEL FACKRE
HARMON L. SMITH
ROBERT W. GLEASON, S.J.
GERALD KENNEDY
JOSEPH FLETCHER

United Church Press · The Bethany Press

The scripture quotations in this publication are (unless otherwise indicated) from the *Revised Standard Version of the Bible,* copyrighted 1946 and 1952 by the Division of Christian Education, National Council of Churches, and are used by permission.

The publishers acknowledge with appreciation permission to quote from the following copyrighted sources:

Thought, for an adapted and abridged form of an article by Robert W. Gleason, "Situational Morality," in Vol. XXXII, 1957.

The Duke Divinity School Review, for an adapted and expanded form of a book review of Joseph Fletcher's *Situation Ethics* by Harmon L. Smith, in Vol. XXXI, no. 2, Spring, 1966.

The Christian Century, for an adapted and expanded form of a book review by James M. Gustafson, "How Does Love Reign?" Copyright 1966 Christian Century Foundation. Reprinted by permission from the May 18, 1966, issue of *The Christian Century.*

The Westminster Press, for *Situation Ethics* by Joseph Fletcher. The Westminster Press. Copyright © 1966, W. L. Jenkins. Used by permission.

Cambridge University Press, for *Soundings,* ed. A. R. Vidler.

Harper & Row, Publishers, for *God's Grace and Man's Hope* by Daniel Day Williams, and *Self-Renewal* by John W. Gardner.

The Macmillan Company, for *Ethics* by Dietrich Bonhoeffer.

Dodd, Mead & Company, for *Orthodoxy* by G. K. Chesterton.

Tom Wolfe, for "Speaking Out: Down with Sin!" *The Saturday Evening Post,* June 19, 1965. Used by permission of Tom Wolfe, % Marvin Josephson Associates, Inc. © 1965 Curtis Publishing Company.

Library of Congress Catalog Card Number 67-19286

Foreword

The new morality, like New College at Oxford University, is by this time hardly new. At least it is not new for scholars and professional ethicists who have during the past decade shaken the subject in the manner that a dog worries the marrow out of a bone.

What is new about the so-called new morality is that the interest has shifted from ivy-covered halls and technical journals to what has now become the sidewalk debate. Today the matter is less a question of adjudication between the conflicting claims of neo-nominalists and neo-realists than it is the matter of addressing irate parents and confused young people about the revolution in ethics that is sweeping over the land.

Perhaps no one individual has done more to precipitate the widespread interest in the new morality today than Prof. Joseph Fletcher of Episcopal Theological School in Cambridge, Massachusetts. For it was his book entitled *Situation Ethics* (Philadelphia: Westminster Press, 1966) that served as a catalyst in the matter. In pointing up the practical issues of the new morality and stating in a popular style the position of an avowedly relativistic situation ethics, Professor Fletcher opened wide to the world the scholarly debate on the new morality. In doing so, he caught the attention of persons from every walk of life—professional *humans*, one might say. His words caught the imagination of many, touching the nerve of concern in family and church, drawing fire from the academic community, and stirring up such a general interest as to lead to the popular pastime known as the sidewalk debate over situation ethics.

In drawing forth widespread interest, Professor Fletcher has also generated a fair amount of scholarly opposition. From educators, church leaders, and various scholars have come critical fusillades from both right and left.

So lively have been the demurrers entered against part or all of situation ethics as Professor Fletcher understands it, that it has seemed well to collect in this volume some alternate points of view to his thesis. After this was done, Professor Fletcher was given an opportunity to offer a brief rebuttal.

The contributors to this volume are all men of outstanding ability who are offering an extraordinary measure of intellectual leadership on the American scene. What they have to say about the latest developments in situation ethics will be of interest to the scholarly community as well as to the larger public. The specific titles and functions of the contributors are identified at the bottom of the various chapter openings.

A major purpose in publishing *Storm over Ethics* is to collect in one resource some of the salient problems that must be faced by modern man in deciding the course of practical action to take on the vast number of day-to-day ethical choices that cannot be avoided and that *will* have their decisions—one way or another.

The Publishers

Contents

1

Principles and the Context

Can ethical principles guide action?

J O H N   C .   B E N N E T T

One of the most debated issues among students of Christian ethics today is the methodological question concerning the relation of the universal or at least broadly based criteria in an ethical judgment to the unique elements in the concrete situation.[1] I am never quite sure what word should be used to denote the universal elements. The words *laws* and *principles* have become such objectionable words in many circles that I should like to find some fresh words. I am speaking, of course, about broadly based objectives that help to determine concrete decisions and other normative criteria which are brought to the concrete situation. It is my view that this whole discussion is a matter of emphasis and that those who try to turn it into an absolute choice between the context *with*

John C. Bennett is president of Union Theological Seminary (New York) and Reinhold Niebuhr Professor of Social Ethics.

1

and the context *without* the use of these objectives or criteria, laws or principles, are creating a situation that is quite unreal. The most absolutist contextualist is sure to make use of bootlegged principles. But more of that later!

Those who represent the emphasis on the context accuse those whom they associate with an ethic of principles of imposing a deductive legalistic ethic on changing situations, on situations in which the human complications are such that principles which are often hardened and one-sided are irrelevant or destructive of concrete values. Often the critics of an ethic of "principles" write as though there were little point in the attempt to articulate the kind of Christian guidance that the church as church can bring to a situation within which it is also necessary to take account of technical issues or issues of prudence growing out of the contingent facts.

Since I am often cited as a peculiarly bad example of this deductive approach, I should explain that I am influenced by my own concrete situation. As a teacher of students who are expecting to preach, who are not themselves to be makers of political or social policy, I have been interested in finding out what kind of ethical guidance is appropriate for ministers to include in preaching or for the church as church to provide for its members. Also, I have often been involved in the preparation of ecumenical reports which must have some relevance for many situations without providing all that is necessary for decision in any situation. This whole process seems to many of the critics highly abstract and sterile. But it is my impression that they take many of its results for granted and build on them.

The trend toward contextual ethics has many sources.

2

One is the recognition of the complexity of the factors entering into concrete decisions. Many of us who are concerned about Christian ethics agree that there is no direct line from Christian faith or ethics to some concrete decisions; that these decisions may involve technical judgments concerning which there is no distinctively Christian guidance; that there are judgments of strategy in relation to the use of power which belong to a different world from that of Christian principles; that many of a Christian's choices are difficult, indeed agonizing, choices between evils, no one of which fits ideal prescriptions. The existentialist mood of the times casts discredit on universal moral structures or universal ethical judgments and is akin to the relativism which is partly a mood also, and partly a true recognition of the enormous variations in human conditions.

An important point of contact between existentialist thinking and Christian ethics is, of course, Rudolph Bultmann. He has done little to illumine the complexities of social ethics. His emphasis upon the moment of decision has seemed to offer an oversimplified shortcut to a Christian ethical judgment. In his study of Bultmann's ethics Thomas Oden emphasizes the extent to which Bultmann assumes that the content of what love for the neighbor means is given to the obedient Christian without ambiguity in the situation. He points out that "Bultmann argues that what the moment demands always becomes clearer with a practical knowledge of precedents and consequents. But decision that takes place in one's actual meeting of his neighbor in the moment is never determined by such knowledge." [2] This indicates that, extreme as Bultmann's thought is in its emphasis on the situation, he does not isolate it completely from generalized ethical understanding. Bultmann's own comment on Oden's exposition presents his one-sided emphasis quite clearly:

> But the Christian faith sees every moment in the light of the "Christ event," in the sense that the Christ event teaches man to *know himself* and above all to know himself as one loved by God, so that henceforth he is able, as one who is loved, to perceive the unambiguous meaning of the demand of God in the concrete situation. To be sure, this knowledge is never secure in itself. But the believer can act, even if his action is a *peccare* as long as he fulfills the *crede fortius*.[3]

That sentence suggests the difficulty of this position. The idea of "unambiguous meaning" is likely to put a Christian on the wrong track. The preoccupation with the subjective condition of the Christian himself is itself a source of temptation to escape from the real problems of life when more than one neighbor is involved. Bultmann's one well-known action in a political situation was his support of the resistance of the church against Hitler, but this was a far more unambiguous decision than those which Christian citizens usually have to face. My own contact with the effects of Bultmann's ethical teaching on the life of the church in recent years has been very limited, but the leaders of the World Council of Churches who are concerned about the problems of church and society have found that Bultmann's influence has caused many churchmen on the European continent to turn away from the complicated issues of political and social ethics. This has been due to the tendency to emphasize issues that fit the interest in Christian subjectivity in the moment of decision more than they do the concern to discover the best objective judgment about complex but fateful matters of political and social policy.

4

More directly influential on the chief exponents of contextual ethics have been Barth and Bonhoeffer. Passages can be quoted from their writings which support this position.

Barth, in defending himself against Brunner's charge that he was inconsistent in acting one way in connection with national socialism and another way in connection with communism says:

> Therefore, the church never thinks, speaks, or acts "on principle." Rather it judges spiritually and by individual cases. For that reason it rejects every attempt to systematize political history and its own part in that history. Therefore it preserves freedom to judge each new event afresh.[4]

Though I think that Barth has made his own neutralism into too much of a system, I agree fully with his main point that it would be quite wrong for a man to transfer his position in regard to national socialism to communism without real openness to the important differences between the two. The inability of most Americans to make the distinction has caused great mischief in our own national feeling and policy in relation to the cold war. There are deeper sources of this emphasis on the situation in Barth, which I find especially in his discussion of the "definiteness of the divine decision." [5] I get the impression that Barth moves too quickly from absolute assurance about God's will in general to absolute assurance about what it means for the particular occasion. This enables him to ignore the task of distinguishing between the Christian ingredients in a decision and those elements about which there is no Christian guidance at all. He swoops with the confidence of Joseph Sittler's gull to the right choice. Or perhaps it is God who swoops and carries him along.

But let no one think that Barth dispenses with princi-

5

ples, universal criteria, laws, or whatever a person may prefer to call what is here intended. It is true he bases these principles on the exegesis of scripture or upon his astonishing analogical method of derivation which is guaranteed to produce any result desired. Take his discussion of the ethic of sex and marriage, of the proper order in the relationship of men and women. Who ever has been able to spin out a greater amount of assured knowledge of the norms for Christian behavior in this area? The splendid essay on "The Christian Community and the Civil Community" [6] is full of principles. From my point of view they are sound ones which are most unsoundly derived. All that is sound is summed up in this sentence:

> The reason why we mentioned many examples was that we wanted to demonstrate that the essence of Christian politics is not a system or a succession of momentary brain-waves but a constant direction, a continuous line of discoveries on both sides of the boundary which separates the political from the spiritual spheres, a correlation between explication and application. [7]

He even goes so far as to admit:

> We have argued not from any conception of "natural law" but from the gospel. It cannot be denied, however, that in the list of examples quoted we have more than once made assertions which have been justified elsewhere on basis of natural law. [8]

These things are well said.

Barth's most extensive discussion of Christian ethics is in the fourth part of his third volume where his methodology provides a mediating position between those who emphasize general principles and those who stress the uniqueness of a situation. On many issues he states the main-line Christian position as he understands it; this is true of the issues surrounding monogamy, the permanence of marriage and divorce, suicide, abortion, euthanasia, killing in self-defense, capital punishment, and war. He develops very strong central guidance in each of these cases and then he admits the existence of exceptional cases. Usually he is able to suggest guidance concerning how an exception may be detected. This itself involves some general principles.

But there is this combination of very clear general Christian guidance and freedom to allow for exceptional situations which require moral judgments that do not come from an application of the general principles. For example, there is a strong Christian case against suicide, but Barth recognizes that there are situations such as the case of a man under torture who is afraid that he may be led to betray his friends. He says that in principle the Christian should renounce the right to kill in self-defense but he allows that this may be commanded by God in a specific case where it is incidental to the defense of the neighbor. But he says, "Even on the outermost limits on which we now find ourselves, it is only on the extreme edge that we can accord this right to the individual." [9] Barth is often too confident that there will be an unambiguous command of God available in these cases. This is most baffling in his discussions of divorce where the command of God seems strangely unrelated to empirical indications concerning the goodness or health of a particular marriage.

Dietrich Bonhoeffer states the case for a strongly contextualist interpretation of Christian ethics:

What can and must be said is not what is good once and for all, but the way in which Christ takes form among us here and now. The attempt to define that which is good once and for all has, in the nature of the case, always ended in failure. Either the proposition was asserted in such general terms that it retained no signifi-

7

cance in regard to its contents, or else it tried to include in it and elaborate the whole immense range of conceivable contents and thus to say in advance what would be good in every conceivable case; this led to a casuistic system so unmanageable that it could satisfy the demands neither of general validity nor of concreteness.[10]

I agree with Bonhoeffer in regard to the systems of casuistry which he describes, but I doubt if he is right in attaching no value to what is asserted in general terms. I think that his book is full of such assertions. Also, I doubt if Christians can dispense with some criteria if they are to decide when "Christ is taking form among us here and now." This can be claimed by Christians in a way that distorts the ethical meaning of Christ. When I say that Bonhoeffer makes use of general considerations which are brought to the concrete situation, I refer to his discussion of the "mandates" in his *Ethics,* to his discussion of the rights of the person, of such matters as euthanasia, of suicide, of birth control. He gives some instruction as to when it is permissible and when it is not permissible to commit suicide.[11] It is interesting that he opposes Roman Catholic moral theology in regard to birth control [12] but seems to uphold it in regard to the competing claims of the life of the fetus and the life of the mother.[13]

One of the most interesting passages in Bonhoeffer's *Ethics* is where he discusses the relationship of a pagan government to the second table of the Ten Commandments. He renounces the concept of "natural law" but says that there is "providential congruity between the contents of the second table and the inherent law of historical life itself." And the knowledge of this inherent law of historical life itself is available to pagan governments. This "inherent law" is at least a substitute for natural law.[14]

8

I have referred in this way to Barth and Bonhoeffer in order to suggest that a contextual ethic completely separated from universal or broadly based normative considerations is not really viable. I think that this can be shown from the writings of anyone who deals constructively with ethical problems and moves beyond a polemic against principles. I shall now seek to clear the way for a discussion of the main problem by suggesting a few misconceptions of what is involved, calling attention to a few things that this issue is not.

This discussion of principles versus the context is not a question concerning the relation between grace and law. I am interested here in the sources of guidance for what Christians should do and not with the fulfillment of the law as a means of salvation. This is not the question as to *when* decisions should be made. They usually should be made in the context. I think that sometimes there is confusion between *guidance* for decisions and motive or energy for decisions; not motive or energy to act on the decision but motive or energy to decide. Often we cannot do this until we are on the spot and cannot evade decision. This forced character of the decision is not itself a source of wisdom but it does cause us to make use of the wisdom that we have. This includes reading the facts of the situation on the spot.

Sometimes the contextual emphasis is presented in such a way that it seems to provide a religious shortcut to wisdom about the situation because of the language that is used. We are exhorted to respond to what God is doing in the situation. (Cf. Bonhoeffer's "the way in which Christ takes form among us here and now.") The interpretation of the situation as a locus of divine action may have a great deal to do with a man's motive and energy

9

for action, but I do not see that it provides any shortcut to wisdom concerning what he should decide to do. To determine what God is doing in the situation is no easier than it is to decide what he should do—though exhortations of this kind often seem to assume that what God is doing is an obvious matter. There is a danger that Christians may identify God's action with the apparent "wave of the future" or that they will be influenced by authoritarian religious criteria.

The question at issue is not identical with that which is involved in the debate over the place of natural law and of revealed knowledge of God's will. In practice, the kind of mind that gives most place to universals is likely to be hospitable to ideas of natural law or to some equivalent of them. But the issue is present also when we seek to relate convictions derived from revelation to the unique occasion.

There is here a special problem in connection with Paul Lehmann's "koinonia ethics." When Christians make decisions about matters of public policy, they usually think and act with non-Christians and so there must be some common moral convictions which guide them. It is useful to be able to state these convictions in terms which are intelligible to non-Christians. These convictions may be derived from revelation ultimately in a society which is strongly influenced by Christianity, but even so they can still be defended by considerations which have a broader base than the Christian revelation. There is operating here at least an equivalent of the idea of "natural law," hopefully an equivalent that is dynamic and that is never allowed to be separated from the commands of love.

In addition to this difficulty that I have with Professor Lehmann's discussion of ethical methodology, I want to raise two other issues at this point. First, I can never tell from his discussion where the koinonia is. I doubt if it is either a particular local church or the total ecumenical community in his view. His very prophetic ethical stance would not fit well with either. If it is a gathered fellowship of a prophetic sort, this would itself be gathered in the light of some criteria. Second, ethical guidance for Lehmann does not come from ethical principles "but from what God is doing in the world to make and to keep human life human." [15] That is an excellent formula but it seems to involve many descriptive and many normative principles as soon as the question is asked what it means to be human and under what conditions men are more likely to become truly human. If Professor Lehmann would develop answers to these questions more systematically, he would almost certainly provide what I feel to be lacking in his formal presentation, for I usually find myself in agreement with his actual conclusions.

THE NECESSITY OF EMPHASIZING THE CONTEXT

I agree with those who emphasize the context and who reject a deductive ethical rationalism or a strict casuistry based upon principles which imply with precision their own application to each situation. My only concern is to spell out more than is sometimes thought necessary what Christians bring to the situation. The facts of situations are different. The opportunities for action are different. The roles of the persons or groups that must make decisions are different. Any situation viewed from inside by those who have responsibility for decision is apt to be different from what it is even to the view of sympathetic but somewhat detached observers. Ethical goals that may be

11

the same in two situations are mixed with technical and strategic considerations which form unique combinations. Often timing is of the essence and this depends upon the most sensitive awareness of changing conditions. Negotiations leading to decisions depend upon the attitudes and opinions of those who happen to be negotiating, and these are part of the data on which the decisions themselves are based, data that cannot be known in advance.

One reason for the great emphasis upon contextual ethics today is that Christians are aware of many decisions involving hard choices which defy the application of any recognized moral principles, and the choice that may seem necessary at a given moment may be so morally repellent that the last thing we want is to have it establish a new principle. We hope to be able to regard it as a moral exception. Large-scale choices of this kind are more fully recognized as a factor in the moral life of Christians today than has been the case in recent centuries. At least there is far greater awareness of them and they are certainly more fateful than ever before in history. The margin of error has been reduced catastrophically by the availability of nuclear weapons. Many decisions on a smaller scale have harassed the consciences of contemporary Christians in the daily conduct of war and in the resistance movements. The weakening of some of the elements in the moral tradition in the Protestant churches has increased the range of options for many Christians in such areas as euthanasia and suicide, but again there would be general hesitancy about precedents and the establishing of new principles. Ad hoc judgments under these circumstances seem in order. However, when Christians make these hard decisions they should do so because of goals which are defensible on the basis of some principles, and should know in the light of what principles the decisions are hard. Otherwise such ad hoc decisions would be absurdly blind and I am sure that no student of Christian ethics intends them to be so.

One of my German students discussed in a term paper the ethical dilemmas of the resistance movement. He said that the objectives of the illegal resistance do not limit the methods. Even the clearest objectives may involve men in the most terrible methods. He wrote:

Some individuals might have started out their illegal activities in order to save Jews from deportation. In order to get them, let us say, to Switzerland they had to forge passports. If they tried to hide them somewhere within the country itself, it usually involved bribing SS men who would cross out the names of the persons to be hidden in the lists of persons to be deported. Identification papers and ration cards had to be forged. In this whole process there were, of course, dozens of opportunities for betrayal or detection. Often the only way to escape either one was to kill the person or persons from whom the threat came. Even more terrible were those situations in which an underground circle knew that detection was threatening from somewhere and also knew the person—perhaps an SS guard—who knew what was being planned against them, and then had to face the decision as to whether or not they should try to obtain this information on which their lives depended by torturing him. All these steps were logical and sometimes inevitable results of the initial decision to save the lives of innocent Jews—nothing more than that.

WHAT CHRISTIANS SHOULD BRING TO THE CONTEXT

I am not attempting here to present the whole range of Christian wisdom that the church and the Christian citizen should bring to the situation. This wisdom includes the acknowledgment in faith that God is the Lord of state and nation and culture and that the surest source of dis-

13

tortion of outlook and of policy is the tendency to absolutize these human realities. Grateful obedience to God, which is understood in terms of love for all neighbors, including enemies and opponents, should be the ultimate determiner of motive in relation to policy. Such love brings its own sensitivities, its own antennae, to the situation. Also we Christians are helped by our confession of our sin and weakness to understand the type of temptation that is likely to distort our minds; we see ourselves and all those against whom we may seem arrayed in the light of a common judgment and a common redemption. Christian awareness of redemption that is embodied in some measure even in the larger communities of men gives meaning to what we do and Christian hope in God's ultimate fulfillment of his purpose for human life brings perspective and freedom from panic in the hardest situations. It is very difficult as we think of these sources of guidance, which come from the redemption of man through Christ, to distinguish between ethical guidance that is relevant to policy and the sources of morale, of attitudes which make policy more tolerable as we seek to implement it. It is my impression that the contextualists tend to slur over this distinction. Sometimes they do so by drawing more guidance for policy from redemption than is available from that source; sometimes they seem to allow a "realistic" dealing with the context to push too far toward the margin of thought the distinctively Christian sensitivities and judgments.

Christians should bring two types of ethical criteria as guidance to each social situation.

Criteria of a somewhat general sort that are relevant to all situations but which do not of themselves determine concrete decisions. These have to do with the broad goals

14

for society. Such goals conflict and for this reason no one of them is a law; it is a guide concerning direction which keeps our decisions from being blind. I refer to such obvious criteria or objectives as order, freedom, justice, the openness of society to truth, the need for productivity or concern for the material conditions of welfare. To mention these is to remain in the realm of the abstract. Each requires careful definition; *there are no universal principles for relating them to one another.* And yet to allow any one of them to drop out as a vital concern from the mind that we Christians bring to the concrete situation would be disastrous. We need to do much thinking in advance about the relation between these criteria or objectives, about their interdependence, even if such thinking cannot produce for us a law. For example, it is important to have some clear ideas about how we arrange order and freedom in terms of priority. Do we or do we not believe that there are times when it may be justifiable to risk the loss of order for the sake of freedom? Do we or do we not also recognize that without the hope of a new order such a risk would be irresponsible? We need to have a clear idea about what constitutes justice before the law and of some of the considerations that go into the determination of justice in relation to economic opportunity or the distribution of wealth. We need to have some convictions about the relation of justice to equality. I am sure that if we make clear that we cannot freeze in advance any precise arrangements of these criteria, no contextualist will oppose what I am saying, but I should emphasize this advance thinking which would include some projection of possible arrangements.

How are these broad criteria related to Christian ethics? I think that they are the ways Christians have of

15

spelling out what the good of the neighbor is in the world as we know it. They cannot be derived from Christian love alone but from Christian love as it seeks knowledge concerning the needs of the community of neighbors. There is a source of guidance concerning Christian ethics which comes neither from the ethical imperatives nor from our contemporary reading of the situation but from Christian teaching concerning man, concerning his relationship to God, his social nature, his depth and freedom as a person, and concerning the relation of all these aspects of man to his sin. For example, all that we think today about freedom is controlled by such considerations as: man is true to himself only when he makes his decisions freely but in obedience to God; in society man's freedom must include his recognition that God transcends all social principalities and powers; man's sinful striving for advantages for himself or his own group makes it necessary to guard other men against exploitation and tyranny and so there must be checks upon all human power, checks that involve some balancing of power.

Whose freedom should concern us? The freedom of all men with special emphasis upon "those least" who cannot defend their own freedom. Always as we think in this way we must learn old lessons over again from contemporary experience and we must be on our guard against new threats to freedom. It makes a great difference whether at a given time we emphasize the threats that come from the church or from the state or from a foreign aggressor or from economic powers or from the pervasive culture.

These broad criteria should lead us to more specific objectives which belong to a particular historical period. In the ecumenical literature, objectives of this sort are sometimes called "middle axioms." These may be objectives or descriptions of some condition of which policy must take account. The overcoming of involuntary racial segregation is a middle axiom in the sense of a normative principle while the judgment that segregation is a form of discrimination is a middle axiom of the descriptive type. I have no interest in perpetuating the phrase middle axiom, but it is important to have some designation of objectives or judgments that have a particular reference to our concrete situation, that are determiners of policy and yet are not identical with the most concrete policy which is the immediate guide to action. Why is it important to distinguish between a middle axiom and a policy? My reason for doing so is that there can often be agreement on these middle axioms when there is no agreement on policy and such agreement may greatly help to form a common mind in church and community which will prepare the way for agreement on policy later. It may prepare the way at least for the acceptance of policy as a fait accompli and such acceptance is essential for the stability of policy. The corporate teaching of the church on controversial social issues is seldom more specific than the projection of so-called middle axioms, but if these do become part of the mind of the church it becomes possible for it more effectively to encourage its members and many voluntary groups to experiment with the support of specific policies.

Desegregation is one of the clearest examples of the kind of objective that needs to be brought to a situation. I shall list several other objectives that have a claim upon us and are ways of expressing ethical criteria for our time which are implied in Christian faith and ethics even though they are not exclusively Christian.

17

- The prevention of general nuclear war.
- The working out of moral limits for the conduct of any military operations.
- The concern for the maintenance or the development of societies, which are marked by openness and pluralism, in which there are protections of spiritual and cultural freedom.
- The acceptance of the responsibility of the nation acting through government to maintain the stability of the economy and to develop the essential conditions of welfare for the whole population.

Often the universal element in the sphere of politics can be seen most clearly in negative terms. Edmond Cahn's emphasis on the fact that man may recognize what is unjust before he can with equal clarity define justice is suggestive.[16] Christians have the task of discovering the implicit standard of justice in their judgment that a particular act is unjust. At the Evanston Assembly of the World Council of Churches there was an effort to spell out various criteria for the "responsible society" and it seemed natural to begin with one obvious evil that has plagued every totalitarian society as the first thing to avoid. With that in mind the first of these criteria was expressed as follows: "Every person should be protected against arbitrary arrest or other interference with elementary human rights." One could argue at length about what these elementary human rights are but any society that does protect its citizens against arbitrary arrest would be at least tolerable in this area.

It may give aid and comfort to the contextualist for me to confess that each time I try to state principles and objectives of this sort I find myself more inclined to stumble. But the stumbling comes not so much from the feeling that such objectives and principles are unimportant as from the realization that in each concrete situation we may have difficulty in relating to each other principles and objectives all of which have a claim upon us. This fact may enable the contextualist to have a field day, but I should not want to be guided by him if I thought that in his decisions he acted with such spontaneity in the immediate situation that he was unaware of the extent to which he was sacrificing one principle or objective to another. Let these principles be internalized and let them become absorbed into the style of life but let them remain capable of being recalled to mind from time to time as reminders of what Christians may be neglecting as well as where they are going. This is more important, the more the immediate situation threatens them.

One of my chief criticisms of Joseph Fletcher's methodology in his interesting and provocative *Situation Ethics* is that he does not provide for the continuing role of a principle, which at the moment he may sacrifice to another principle. After stating that there are important rules, maxims, principles which illuminate ethical problems, he says that the situationist "is prepared in any situation to compromise them or set them aside *in the situation* if love seems better served by doing so." [17] Elsewhere in this book there will be a full discussion of the inadequacy of assuming that love itself is the ultimate norm that displaces other norms.[18] Love that seeks the welfare of the neighbor must be guided by norms that indicate the content of such welfare. My chief concern is to insist that we in deciding do not set aside an important principle. It may be subordinated to another, but the way in which we act will be determined in part by the subordinated principle. For example, if we decide that we must support the use of military force and in so doing sacrifice peace to justice, we need to keep the use of such force under severe criticism. The continuing emphasis on the limits within which force should be used is a result of the continuing relevance of principles that Fletcher may think he has set aside. He may think that the word compromise covers what is needed, but his way of stating the problem tends to be too unguarded at this point.

Let me illustrate the tension between principles and objectives by referring to two areas of decision that are continually in our minds. There is a real tension between the prevention of nuclear war and the deterrence of aggression. If there were no threat of aggression or blackmail, we could easily avoid many policies that may become provocative and may even lead to limited military operations which could escalate into general nuclear war. This is a good example of the need to relate contrasting objectives within the same situation. There must be much "playing by ear." Many decisions which cannot be charted in advance have to be made, but let us hope that the decision-makers never abandon deep concern for either objective. They may have to decide in advance if either objective should have some degree of priority, but even this is not likely to be settled finally in advance of all concrete occasions. Some considerations seem to have been neglected, and greater attention to them might change the sense of priorities as future decisions are made.

I have in mind three considerations that should guide us in the face of this dilemma and I shall mention them not for their own sake but in order to illustrate the way we should think about a problem of this kind. (1) There is the opportunity that we have now in being able to distinguish between the various communist countries. Some of the panic can go out of the cold war as we recognize that communism is not a monolithic international force which threatens to isolate increasingly those nations which belong to the so-called free world. There is now much more room for diplomatic maneuvering and for establishing helpful relations with many communist countries. The tendency to see the world in black-and-white terms should belong to the past. (2) Partly because communism no longer means permanent "slavery" in contrast to "freedom," we can say that a general nuclear war would be the worst fate that could befall humanity, that it would probably destroy the institutions of freedom in a more deadly way and with less chance for a comeback for them than would communism. To say this does not settle all the problems of policy in the context of deterrence but it does suggest how inadequate deterrence is as a protection of humanity. It helps to reveal a moral imperative to find a way that goes beyond the deterrence pattern of the cold war. (3) We should emphasize more than we do the risks in the continuation of the arms race itself and realize that there is no full security either in radical disarmament or in the holding up of the American end in the arms race.

A second illustration has to do with the vexing question of the universal relevance of democratic institutions. Increasingly as we observe the actual conditions in many nations, it seems clear that often order must be stressed at the expense of freedom and that regimes which appear to us to be authoritarian or even semitotalitarian may have to be accepted. Against the idealist who insists that democracy as we know it in the West must be exported to all countries before we will accord them our moral approval, we must emphasize the need of great flexibility in

21

the development of political institutions in other nations. To insist that they have opposition parties and parliaments which function as though they had had generations of democratic experience as background is obviously absurd. Yet we do not go so far as to say that one political system is as good as another for any country. Nations which must begin with strongly authoritarian governments should become aware that it is good to have some degree of pluralism in a nation, that it soon becomes intolerable for the human spirit if the only effective power or influence in a nation is that of the state or if the state itself never learns to accept limits to its authority. A transitional dictatorship is always tempted to be more than transitional; it should never be made to appear that it is good for this to happen in any country. Everywhere freedom for the mind and the spirit is a great good to be sought, and no situational relativism should be allowed to obscure this. Moreover, the opportunity for all sections of the population to be able to participate in political life is a great good. If it is not possible at a given stage, so much the worse. This is not a matter of indifference, because any part of the community that has no means of political expression is almost certain to be exploited by other parts of the community. Without insisting that our Western institutions are universal, we can insist that there are elements in what we call democracy which should be present in some form as soon as possible in a society that is to be protected against a dehumanizing tyranny. It may be difficult to spell out in advance exactly what these elements are, but we should never stop trying to do so. Christians in countries with any degree of freedom whatsoever should put their minds on this problem and help one another across all the lines which divide them, as far as this

22

is possible. Common problems and needs and aspirations and goods and dangers and miseries exist, and thought about these should not be determined only by the pressures of one concrete situation. I am sure that there is no contextualist who assumes that they should be so determined but it would be well for them to be clearer about the matter.

The finding of ways of reconciling objectives that are in some measure in conflict does belong to the context. It involves judgments about timing, about the nuances of policy and tactics which can only come within the situation. If we look at the problem of decision again in the light of this tension between objectives, we find that what actually takes place is a narrowing of the morally defensible alternatives. There are boundaries within which action takes place that can be discerned in the light of what we bring to the concrete situation. We do not enter that situation blind or equipped only with a commitment to find the will of God within it. We bring to the situation guidance of the kind that I have tried to illustrate, guidance which does not of itself dictate policy because of this very fact that policy is an effort to do justice to more than one objective, that it must take account of two or more considerations which are in some measure in conflict. I cannot emphasize too much that we need to know as much as we can about the price we pay in terms of one objective as we seek to do justice to another. This prevents the blindness that I have warned against. It is no small thing to recognize the boundaries within which we must act. If new situations develop that make it necessary to push back the boundaries in one direction or another, we should know what we are doing and count the cost,[19] and seek new ways of compensating for it.

23

TWO DANGERS TO BE AVOIDED

We may see the issues involved in this debate over ethical method if we consider two quite different dangers on which those on opposite sides tend to concentrate.

The first is the danger of a single-track devotion to one ethical principle. This can be very destructive and it is a common weakness of American political thinking. Sometimes the emphasis upon freedom is of this character—but so is devotion to many an idealistic cause or the condemnation of many an embodiment of evil. One illustration of this single-track approach is opposition to trade with communist countries because of the judgment that elements of communism are evil. This involves relations with governments and their agents that are judged to be dictatorial or tyrannical or that have particular acts of terror in their past which count against them. One trouble with this kind of judgment is that we do have relations with other governments which have many of the same faults but which are on the right rather than on the left. As for terror, its presence in such a variety of places where there is political tumult is one of the most deeply disturbing realities of our time. We can think, for example, of the massacre of hundreds of thousands of Communists or those alleged to be sympathizers with communism in the recent upheaval in Indonesia, which gave so much satisfaction to "our side." More important is the hope that trade with communist nations will help to tear down the iron curtain and encourage communication between the two worlds (or three worlds). Also, there is today a trend toward moderation in some communist countries which will be strengthened by such relationships and also by the improvement of internal conditions that such trade would favor. At least these other considerations are important and this issue must not be settled by the one judgment that we should have no dealings with governments of which we disapprove.

The other danger is that if we put all our emphasis on the situation, we may be determined too much by the limitations that it places upon our vision. Often what is most needed is for those who are deeply involved in a particular situation to be confronted by experiences and broad religious and ethical interpretations which come from outside the situation. Often a local or a regional unit of the church is the part of the koinonia that is most determined by a particular culture. I believe that this makes it very important for the larger units of the church, which include many types of experience and diverse cultural pressures, to bring guidance to the smaller units. This is the value of the ecumenical efforts to develop a type of Christian teaching that may not fit any situation perfectly and yet have relevance for all situations.

The Christian in bringing this teaching to the particular context in which he must make his concrete decisions cannot apply it by means of a rationalistic legalism. But it may greatly influence the way in which he does his thinking about his own concrete problem. It may often be necessary for any group of Christians whose minds are formed by the pressures of their own immediate environment with its distinctive and perhaps peculiarly baffling problems to be disturbed by the judgments of those who live in quite different situations. By emphasizing this conviction I think that we may show how to do justice to the valid concerns of those who stress principles and of those who stress the situation.

2

Love Monism

How does love reign?

J A M E S   M .   G U S T A F S O N

Morality necessarily consists of *acts*. Most moral judgments that men make refer to their own actions or the actions of others. They judge the consequences of an action to be good or bad; they judge the means used in an action to be right or wrong; they judge the motive for an action to be better or worse; they judge the values that seem to be governing an action to be adequate or inadequate. Acts are always specific. An individual might have a general theory of action, or he might discern persistent patterns of action, but every act is by nature specific. Since an act is specific, it takes place in a *situation*. It takes place in a particular time, in a particular place, and with particular people, things, powers, and ends involved.

James M. Gustafson is chairman of the Department of Religious Studies at Yale University, New Haven, Connecticut, and professor of Christian ethics at Yale Divinity School.

Thus all morality is "situational." Since all morality is situational, every comprehensive theory of morality (ethics) has to take into account the significance of the situation in action.

In terms of the current warped controversy, no one would call Thomas Aquinas a "situational ethicist," for he is generally thought of as one who has a theory of the derivation and content of natural laws that in turn govern and guide men in their particular decisions. However, he is concerned not only with natural-law principles but also with the nature of actions and how the moral man perceives which action is correct in relation to a particular time and place, persons and powers. Since he is concerned with the nature of acts, he is concerned with situations in which acts occur. Obviously, then, the use of the term situation ethics cannot refer to every theory that accounts for the function of situations in decisions and actions. If it did, it would distinguish nothing, for all morality is situational, and an all-comprehensive theory of morality has to account for the significance of the actual situations about which decisions are made, and in which actions occur.

Moral actions involve *judgments* about which is right and wrong, what is good and bad, what is better and worse. Decisions necessarily refer to choices; if there were no options, there would be no decisions. Insofar as decisions are moral, they involve a process of moral evaluation. The process of evaluation makes reference to matters other than the facts of the situation. The actor decides what he *ought* to do, not simply on the basis of what is occurring, but on other bases that are partially if not totally independent of what is occurring. He refers to some commitments, principles, values, and rules in determining

27

what he ought to do in a particular situation. He may ask himself, "What action expresses and maintains my sense of personal integrity in that situation?" Or he may remind himself that he ought to seek the greatest good for the greatest number, deciding thus on the basis of that operating normative moral principle. Or he may ask, "What does self-denying love require?" If he does, he refers to something he is committed to, or values; namely, love. Or he may say to himself that the one thing all morally sensitive people agree upon is that everyone ought to do that which causes the least possible suffering. Then he must decide the course of action in the situation which would do that.

Thus all morality refers to "principle" if that word can be used loosely to include commitments, values, rules of conduct, or other points of reference that exist independent of the particular situation in which the actor exists. No moral act is determined solely by the situation unless there is implicitly or explicitly a commitment to the principle that I ought simply to acquiesce passively to the course of events that seems to be taking place, because such passive acquiescence is right and achieves the good. Even this requires some interpretation of what actually is taking place, what the situation really is. Nor has any moral act occurred if an individual has only speculated about the principle to which he adheres. Acts occur when principles are brought to bear in the determination of what ought to occur in a situation, when moral judgment occurs, and when there is an exertion of the will in the light of that judgment.

CONTRASTING VIEWPOINTS

The recent writings of Paul Ramsey and Joseph Fletcher seem to represent extremes in American Christian ethical theory; Fletcher seems to represent "situational ethics," and Ramsey seems to represent "ethics of principles." Yet, I believe that neither of these two authors would disagree with what has been written in the preceding paragraphs. This is why I have argued elsewhere that it is not fruitful to set up a debate between these two points of view.[1] The issues that separate such writers as Fletcher and Ramsey are more complex and require more refined analysis than popular slogans permit.

One way to find out what divides such authors is to ask two questions. How does one make moral judgments? What commitments, values, rules, or principles are normative, and therefore decisive, in determining the actual content of a judgment and an action? On these two questions there is dispute between Fletcher and Ramsey, as anyone who reads their recent works with only a little care will readily see. There is also, in my judgment, some confusion of these two questions in the writings of each.

The first question is that of *method* in judgment-making; it is relatively neutral with reference to whether one favors war or peace, fornication or chastity. "Situational ethics" can be carefully and strictly construed to refer to a method of making judgments. In the moral equation higher valence is given in principle to what actually seems to be occurring in the time and place in which the moral man exists. But this principle of higher valence does not in itself dictate what one will do in the situation. I may say that it is important in making judgments to take very seriously what is actually occurring. What is occurring

29

may be construed by me as follows: There is a lonely woman, who seems to be in need of a human relationship. Given the importance of knowing that the person is lonely and female does not determine whether I *ought* to become her friend or her sexual lover, whether the love I offer her is philia or libido. The method does not determine the content of the act.

Similarly, "ethics of principles" can be carefully and strictly construed to refer to a method of making judgments. Higher valence is given in principle to the clarification of rules and to the rational determination of conduct. But to give higher valence to clarification of rules and rationality does not dictate *what* I will do. What I will do depends upon the normative content of the rules to which I adhere, to the values to which I am committed. A person can be a principled pacifist or a principled killer; the debate between two such individuals would not be over whether principles are important, but *what* principles are important. One can be in principle chaste; another can be in principle a seducer, and each can be equally rational in the exercise of his principles. It is the normative substance of one's principles and values that makes the difference.

The ways in which particular normative content is wedded to particular methods does, however, seem to make a good bit of difference as to where the moral question comes out. Interestingly, both Ramsey and Fletcher say that, for Christians, "love" is the norm. Indeed, Fletcher calls love, among other things, a "formal principle"; and Ramsey for years has been concerned to "in-principle" love, and to see how "in-principled love" is brought to bear on specific situations and moral judgments. "Love" is a key word for each author. When one

30

reads Fletcher's *Situation Ethics* and Ramsey's *Deeds and Rules in Christian Ethics,* it is useful to keep certain questions in mind. Do these authors use the word they share in common, love, in the same way? Does it have the same or different implications for each? These questions ought to alert the reader to differences in the normative substance of their two views, even though they share the same word. Further, what is it that makes love plus Fletcher's "situational method" sound so radical (in addition to the author's style and announcement that he is radical)? What is it that makes love plus Ramsey's method of rules and principles sound somewhat conservative? Is the difference simply between "act-agapism" (Fletcher) and "rule-agapism" (Ramsey), to use William Frankena's distinctions that Ramsey adopts and cherishes?

SITUATION ETHICS RADICAL?

Among many reasons why Fletcher's situation-plus-love ethic appears to be radical, a few are of great importance. First, he is passionate in his distress at any sign of legalism, actual or potential. His reasons for this are sound enough: He does not want the moral subject to avoid personal responsibility by taking recourse to rules or tradition; he does not want the openness and fluidity of life to be straitjacketed into rules. The effect of this antilegalism is to make Fletcher appear radically relativistic. Thus for the moment one loses sight of a possible modified act-agapism that is in effect a modified rule-agapism.

Second, Fletcher states that the situation is determinative. However, he never really designates what constitutes a situation. Most of the occasions for the most radical of his statements are strictly and narrowly interpersonal; the

31

time-and-space span of relationships is highly limited. If the situation is the determining factor in what love requires, it is terribly important how one interprets his situation. In the interpretation, evaluations are already taking place. Is it boy plus girl between 1 A.M. and 3 A.M. after a number of drinks in a motel room who feel affection for each other stimulated by proper knowledge of erogenous zones? Or is it boy, responsible to others than the girl, and responsible to and for her over a long period of time under a covenant of some sort, plus girl concerned not only for the present moment but also for the past and future relationships, in a human community for whose vitality and order they have responsibility and which in turn has to seek its common good? The minimal facts may be the same: boy, girl, drinks, motel; the interpretation of what the situation *is* differs. When Fletcher moves from interpersonal ethics to social ethics, he becomes a straight utilitarian. He does not argue his point; here as elsewhere he simply asserts it.[2]

Third, Fletcher seems to want an ethic that omits any possibility of a bad conscience. He has unwarranted confidence in the directing and informing power of love. He does take back, however, some of what he seems to give in this regard, for much of the book stresses the fact that love calculates, it extends itself in prudence, it uses principles (not rules) to illumine the case at hand. He wishes to distinguish himself from antinomian ethics or existential ethics as well as from legalism. He really wants to modify his act-agapism; but he does not want people wallowing in guilty feelings for having made moral mistakes.

At this juncture one of the major points of difference between the two authors becomes clear. The authority each grants to various principles or points of consideration in the judgment process differs. Each derives somewhat different inferences from love, and each gives these different weights. Ramsey is concerned for order, for the validity of summary rules that serve love, and for rational clarity in judgment-making. Fletcher says that persons are to be valued most highly, that love is the only intrinsic good, but also that the situation determines what is to be done. Neither author keeps clear the distinction between norm and method.

"Love," like "situation," is a word that runs through Fletcher's book like a greased pig (if I may be excused an allusion to my rural county-fair past). Nowhere does Fletcher take the trouble to indicate in a systematic way his various uses of it. It refers to everything he wants it to refer to. It is the *only* thing that is intrinsically good; it *equals* justice; it is a formal *principle,* it is a *disposition,* it is a *predicate* and not a property, it is a ruling *norm.* This raises grave logical confusions, which will not be dealt with here. More important for this essay, one finds nothing like the delineation of love that H. Richard Niebuhr gave in *The Purpose of the Church and Its Ministry.*[3] If a person says that the situation plus love makes for the right action without being clear about what love is and is not, he has a simple formula, a radical ethic in both substance and method. If he says that love uses its head, he may not have such a radical method and substance. Fletcher wants it both ways, and he cannot have it both ways. A much more careful set of distinctions than he is willing to use would modify the shock effect he wishes to create. He wants to simplify and complicate at once, while generally professing to simplify. On each specific judgment he makes about each specific case he uses, one can argue whether he has rightly considered certain factors such as other "principles" than love and the complexity of the situation. He suggests that moral philosophers who make distinctions between deontological and teleological ethics unduly complicate the matter; yet in the end he says, "Only the end validates the means," and he uses distinctions like realist-nominalist, intrinsicalist-extrinsicalist, and others that lend no argumentative weight to his assertions. Ramsey's critique of Fletcher is implicit in his review of Fletcher's cohort John A. T. Robinson to be found in chapter three of *Deeds and Rules in Christian Ethics*.

If Fletcher is not as radical as he sounds in method or substance, what makes him appear radical? Partly verbal pyrotechnics. But finally, in specific cases he makes what many would believe to be a radical judgment; for example, on abortion, "No unwanted child ought to be born." Whose wants are considered? Is "wanting" always the same thing? Many a mother on a day of misery during pregnancy wishes she were not having that child. Is that the day she decides for an abortion? What if a person says that the formal principle of love is significant even when he does not feel like loving? Fletcher says it is. Then the fetus that I may not feel like loving now is yet to be loved and has a right to exist. Here Fletcher would probably say the fetus is not a person; indeed, on this kind of a case as well as in euthanasia, which Fletcher advocates elsewhere, everything hinges on when a being is and is not a person. All ethics are happiness ethics, he says at one point. This may indicate more of Fletcher's basic moral commitment than many other things he says. Does the right come out of an equation "situation plus love using its head equals our happiness in the moment"? This is too simple. But gone are obligations, duty, self-denial in discipleship to the crucified Lord, concern for order (to have this concern is almost equated with legalism by Fletcher, which we have seen is bad). Gone is the daily repentance of man under God's judgment, man who knows he does not do the good he ought to do.

What makes Ramsey's "rule-agapism" seem conservative in comparison to Fletcher's "act-agapism"? Ramsey critically dissects the Quaker report on sex, Paul Lehmann's ethics, Bishop Robinson's ethics, and H. A. Williams' famous comment about the film *The Mark*:

> Will he be able to summon up the necessary courage or not? When he does, and they sleep together, he has been made whole. And where there is healing, there is Christ, whatever the church may say about fornication. And the appropriate response is—Glory to God in the highest.[4]

(I cannot refrain from speculating about how busy Christ was healing the weekend of the prom activities at my university, as men—it is always men—summoned up the courage to fornicate; and I am sure few of them thought about singing "Glory to God in the highest." Maybe we should have remembered this work of Christ in our prayers of thanksgiving the following Sunday morning.) Ramsey, using the Frankena distinctions, has done in his own ponderous style a critical analysis of some sloppy thinking in these documents that ought to be carefully considered without prejudice by the "new morality" enthusiasts. To be critical of radicals even in their methods is enough these days to make a man appear conservative. But method of thought does not dictate moral content.

The difference lies partly in the way Ramsey moves from agape (I disagree with love monism in Christian ethics, whether it comes from Cambridge or Princeton or anywhere else) to the situation of moral action, in the inference he draws from love. Let us work a hypothetical case. "Love your neighbor." This may, for Fletcher, mean, "Be concerned about her person in the situation; love using its head may say, 'fornicate.'" Ramsey would probably say: "Love is concerned not only with the neighbor's need but also with *how* that need is to be met. Love has reference to means, as well as to ends. Now, moral experience and reflection in the Christian community has come up with some specifications and generalizations about how love of neighbor is to be enacted. You are not the first person who has thought about how the neighbor is to be loved. The general and summary rules that have come from Christian reflection have authority; certainly among them is this: Love of neighbor in all but the most exceptional circumstances rules out fornication. These rules do not exist by some arbitrary authority; they are not the ossification of tradition. Love of the person is not absolutely unique in every situation; there is a structure to human relationships that sustains love. Situations are larger and more complex than some people would like to make them appear, and from reflection on the meaning of love becoming in-principled, we can find rules that guide behavior in particular occasions." Methodologically it is not the situation alone that determines but also the operating principles that determine what an individual ought to do in the situation. Substantively when love is worked out in the form of general and summary rules, we find out what it restricts as well as what it permits. For Ramsey too, persons act in situations, and responsibility is theirs. But they may do what is wrong, as well as what is right.

One always has to ask if Ramsey fully appreciates the

freedom of the Christian to do the unusual in loving the neighbor. The problem is not that he espouses rules for rules' sake; he wants rules for the sake of love and persons. But is moral judgment-making as rational as he suggests? Neither author attends to the role of sensitivity, affections, and imagination in moral decisions—things rightly brought into the picture by Paul Lehmann.

Deeds and Rules in Christian Ethics and *Situation Ethics* could be reviewed together with a very different concern in mind; namely, the contribution of each to the academic study of Christian ethical thought. Ramsey's series of reviews (for this is what his book is) is significant, particularly his last chapter in which he deals with Frankena's important work, but so is his long essay on Lehmann. This is not the place to evaluate Ramsey's judgments of these men. Fletcher's book adds less than I had hoped it would, for there is little careful argument. It is made up too much of assertions, observations, preachments, stale jokes, significant cases that could have been the subject of more extensive arguments, sometimes dubious historical allusions (for example, can one quote Augustine's "Love God, and do what you please," while at the same time attacking the theory of the virtues that makes the statement significant in Augustine's framework?), and loose use of words. But Fletcher is easier to read, more sprightly, and will get a wide reception.

I wish every reader who reads one would read the other. For both writers, love is king; how he reigns, however, makes a lot of moral difference.

37

3

Responsibility in Freedom

What is the ethical situation?

E. CLINTON GARDNER

The terms *situation ethics, new morality,* and *contextual ethics* have become catchwords in contemporary discussions of Christian ethics. As such they reflect the prevailing mood of our present-day culture both in its revolt against authority, including traditional moral standards, and in its focus upon the freedom of the individual, upon change, and upon the primacy of immediately personal values. Since situation ethics generally, as this term is currently used, is largely conditioned by the contemporary revolt against authority and tradition and since it is essentially an ethic of unstructured freedom, it is likely that as the study of Christian ethics advances and the understanding of the social nature of man deepens, this form of ethics will, as one writer suggests, prove to be the

E. Clinton Gardner is professor of Christian ethics at the Candler School of Theology, Emory University, Atlanta, Georgia.

"ethics of a transitory situation" or "an interim ethic." [1] Indeed, there is increasing evidence that the inadequacies of this type of ethics are already being recognized by some of its leading representatives.[2]

The primary purpose of this essay is to describe an alternative interpretation of Christian ethics, not to present a critique of contextualist ethics generally or even of Joseph Fletcher's *Situation Ethics* in particular. However, since the stimulus for the current discussions on ethics was provided by the appearance of Professor Fletcher's book, it will be helpful to indicate at the outset the relationship between that book and the position represented here. I shall turn, first of all, to an analysis of some of the major issues raised by Fletcher, focusing attention upon the most important differences between these respective interpretations of ethics. Against this background an effort will be made to describe in summary form the position which, I believe, provides a more adequate basis for understanding man's moral activity from the standpoint of Christian faith than does Fletcher's situationism.

There are many different types of contextual, or situation, ethics, and each of these positions needs to be evaluated in terms of its own particular strengths and weaknesses. However, for purposes of the present analysis, I shall focus attention upon certain issues raised by Fletcher in his important and provocative book.

METHOD VERSUS CONTENT

According to Fletcher, the basic question in ethics is that of method rather than that of the normative content of an ethical choice. Hence the primary focus of *Situation Ethics* is upon the question: How should a Christian go about making a moral decision? [3] Fletcher contends that there are basically only three possible answers to this question; namely, the legalistic, the antinomian, and the situational. He opts for the last of these, and the remainder of his book is largely devoted to a description of this method—the working presuppositions upon which the position is based and six key propositions designed to "show how love works" in making ethical decisions. [4]

While the question of method is crucial in ethics, morality is also concerned with the substantive content—the values, the responsibilities, the commitments, the principles—of ethical decision-making and moral activity. One of the major purposes of ethical reflection is to shed light on the question of what is at stake in a moral choice. The greatest weakness of *Situation Ethics* is found at precisely this point: its failure to deal seriously with the need for clarification of the substantive content and meaning of moral choices and for direction in decision-making.

Fletcher is primarily concerned with emphasizing the freedom of man in the ethical situation. The "new morality" provides the moral agent with a charter of freedom and places upon him the entire responsibility for determining in the situation what it means to love the neighbor. In a sense, therefore, Fletcher's book is pre-ethics or metaethics, for it fails to come to grips with the real ethical issues involved in moral situations in which the choices are complex and morally ambiguous. In the cases that he gives for purposes of stimulating ethical reflection, it is not sufficient simply to tell the reader "to love persons"; some guidance is needed at the point of helping the moral agent discover what it means to love the neighbor in those situations in which many conflicting values and loyalties are at stake.

40

THREEFOLD TYPOLOGY

Fletcher maintains that there are basically only three approaches to decision-making: the legalistic, the antinomian, and the situational. For the legalist the answer to every moral choice is provided by "prefabricated rules and regulations"; it can be discovered, not by an examination of the moral situation itself, but by the application of the right rule or law. The antinomian, however—whether of the libertine, the Gnostic, or the existentialist variety—rejects all principles and rules and relies entirely upon each situation to provide its own ethical solution. The situationist rejects both of these approaches. He uses maxims and principles to illuminate the moral situation, but he is not bound by them; he recognizes only one absolute requirement, that of love.

It is ironic that a book on the methodology of ethics should be based upon such an inadequate typology of the methods which are actually employed in decision-making. By limiting the opposition to what are, in effect, straw men—namely, legalism and antinomianism—Fletcher gains much too easy a victory for the situational approach to ethics. It is difficult to discover after the battle is over just who has been banished from the field and, indeed, who has won the day! For situation ethics assumes many different guises, ranging all the way between the polar opposites of legalism and antinomianism; and almost any real-life ethicist can qualify as a situationist, although some are obviously more typical of this position than others.

As a result of this greatly simplified typology, Fletcher groups together such a wide range of contemporary ethi-

41

cal thinkers—including Barth, Bonhoeffer, Brunner, H. Richard Niebuhr, Joseph Sittler, James M. Gustafson, Paul Lehmann, and Paul Tillich—under the umbrella of situationalism that the label becomes practically meaningless for purposes of precise methodological analysis. Moreover, none of the critics of situational ethics whom Fletcher mentions among American Protestant Christians is a legalist in the sense in which he uses the term: "Not just the spirit but the letter of the law reigns." [5]

Fletcher himself seems to recognize the inadequacy of this threefold typology. On the one hand, he declares that "Judaism, Catholicism, Protestantism—all major Western religious traditions have been legalistic," [6] and he speaks of the "basic legalism of classical Christian ethics." [7] On the other hand, he writes: "It may well be, on careful thought, that in effect most men are situationists and always have been!" [8] Again, he declares, "Historically, most men really have been situationists, more or less." [9] But it is just the differences included in this "more or less"—not just the relatively rare legalism and antinomianism—that call for more precise analysis.

Putting the issue another way, if one assumes that the focal point of ethics should be and generally is upon concrete situations rather than upon abstract rules or an equally abstract autonomous self, what is needed is more attention to different ways of analyzing the ethical situation itself; for the situationists to whom Fletcher refers obviously differ a great deal among themselves in this regard. It is a matter of relative indifference whether one places Brunner in the situationist camp or not; the important thing is to see how Brunner understands the moral life of the Christian in relationship to a variety of problems and issues—and how he does so in terms of

42

polarities (in *Justice and the Social Order*[10]) as well as in terms of a single love commandment (in *The Divine Imperative*[11]).

AGAPE, SELF-LOVE, AND UTILITARIANISM

The same lack of precision that is found in Fletcher's typology of approaches to decision-making is also present in his analysis of love and value. He has many important things to say about the nature of Christian love. For example, love is an attitude, not a feeling; it pertains to the will or disposition.[12] Hence, love "wills the neighbor's good whether we like him or not."[13] Moreover, love is the ruling norm in decision-making, and its "decisions are made situationally, not prescriptively."[14]

Fletcher is quite sensitive to human need, and he is quite correct in defending the final autonomy of love. But he does not make it clear what love means or how it is related to other virtues. Agape, he declares, is the Christian requirement for man in relation to God just as it is between man and man.[15] To say this, however, is to overlook the clarification of the meaning of agape in relation to eros and the different qualities of love that are appropriate for man in relation to God as distinguished from neighbor-love, found in other writers.[16]

To say with Fletcher that, while agape is essentially other-regarding, it has a place for self-love for the neighbor's sake[17] is semantically confusing. For, if agape is essentially neighbor-centered, it must remain so when it is concerned with the self for that reason; and such concern for the self is not really self-love but neighbor-love because its primary center is the neighbor and not the self. Neighbor-love is consistent with self-acceptance and self-

43

respect, but it is inconsistent with self-centeredness or selfishness.[18]

In the area of social ethics, Fletcher equates love with the utilitarian principle of the "greatest good for the greatest number,"[19] and he interprets this formula variously to mean "the greatest amount of neighbor welfare for the largest number of neighbors possible,"[20] the greatest amount of happiness,[21] and "what is most 'useful' for the most people."[22] Such a conception of love, however, overlooks the more distinctively Christian understanding of agape as an act that is directed essentially toward the service of the greatest need of even "the least" of humanity.

The lack of clarity and precision in Fletcher's understanding of agape is due in large measure to his love monism; that is, to his tendency to reduce all virtues to love. While love is not itself a virtue,[23] it is the quality which makes "all other 'virtues'" good. But instead of transforming and using other virtues which have their place in the manifold interpersonal and social relationships of men with each other (as Augustine, for example, did), Fletcher *equates* love with justice and prudence. In effect, he substitutes love for justice—and indeed for all other "virtues." Such love monism obscures the tension between the competing claims and values present even in one-to-one relationships but more especially in the more complex relationships of community life generally. As Aristotle saw, there are many excellencies which pertain to the various faculties and potentialities of man; and, as Augustine saw, the proper relationship of love to these "natural" virtues is that of converting them, or transforming them, by directing them toward their proper end: love for God rather than love for the self. Fletcher's re-

44

ductionism of all virtues to love thus obscures the polarities of ethical experience generally; in particular, it fails to provide an adequate basis for a responsible social ethic. In this regard Emil Brunner, whom Fletcher considers to be a situationist largely on the basis of what he says about love in the earlier portions of *The Divine Imperative*, has a much stronger basis for a social ethic in his concept of the "orders of creation" in the same book and also in his recognition of the polar relationships between justice and love in *Justice and the Social Order.*

GUILT OR ERROR?

A fourth issue that Fletcher raises in his analysis of situation ethics concerns guilt. This issue is directly related to his apprehension of love as goodwill and to his personalistic and ahistorical understanding of man's moral situation. While accepting Reinhold Niebuhr's view of the relativity of love, Fletcher rejects his definition of agape as essentially sacrificial love typified by Jesus' giving of himself on the cross. Niebuhr, he believes, turns love into a transcendent ideal or property which lies beyond the realm of human attainment. For Niebuhr, Christian love is an absolute norm which always lies on the edge of history and is related to human conduct only in a dialectical way as history's "impossible possibility." For Fletcher, however, love is a descriptive, or predicate, term which refers to a situationally defined goodwill, and its limits are set by the presently existing situation. In a word, agape requires only the willing of the greatest good for the greatest number in a particular situation at a given time, and it includes some measure of self-love along with love for the neighbor. The supreme requirement of

45

Christian love is: "Do what you can where you are." [24] Moreover, for Fletcher, the ethical quality of an act is determined entirely by the motivation underlying the act. Hence, he is led to reject both the neo-Protestant concept of the universality of human sinfulness and the more restricted notion (which he associates with John Bennett) that in some situations the best available choice is the "lesser evil"; for love requires only that one will the greatest possible good for the greatest number under the presently existing circumstances.

In those tragic situations in which suffering and injury to some are the necessary but indirect consequences of willing the greatest good for the largest number, the moral agent ought not to experience a sense of guilt, according to Fletcher, but rather a feeling of "sorrow" or regret.[25] Similarly, since man is finite, he may actually choose a course of action which does not promote the greatest amount of human welfare; however, this failure in itself should not become the occasion of remorse but simply of regret since it involves only an "error" of judgment.

Fletcher's tendency to substitute the category of "sorrow" for "guilt" reflects a basically Greek understanding of the tragic in terms of fate rather than a biblical understanding of evil in historical terms; his tendency to substitute "error" for "sin" in his analysis of the consequences of objectively wrong choices reflects a Greek understanding of evil in terms of "missing the mark," rather than in terms of man's distorted or twisted will. Yet Fletcher can never really discard the more profound biblical and Lutheran understanding of the depth of man's involvement in guilt; for he recognizes that the believer, seeking to spend himself in love's work, must finally, in Luther's phrase, "sin bravely." [26] Obviously, here this phrase implies a concept of guilt which runs deeper than consciously intended goodwill. The first mate on the ill-fated *William Brown*, who threw a number of men out of a longboat into the sea in order to save the remaining passengers, Fletcher says, did a "bravely sinful" and "good" thing.[27] Or, again, he cites Monsarrat's picture of the destroyer commander in the novel *The Cruel Sea* as a perfect picture of Luther's *pecca fortiter*. With the commander of the destroyer, Fletcher affirms that "there are times when all we can do is guess our best, and then get down on our knees and ask God's mercy." [28] If the only measure of the moral quality of an act were its present motivation, the term sin would be inappropriate in describing the choice of the best available alternative; but this term alone is finally adequate precisely because it points to man's responsibility for the limited alternatives which are presently available and to the moral agent's involvement in this responsibility (and guilt) as a social being. The language of sin points to the moral agent's real though limited responsibility both for his own moral limitations, which limit his understanding of the moral situation as well as his own ability to "guess" his best, and for the situation itself.

Fletcher's aversion to guilt is closely related to his aversion to law and principles and, indeed, to every effort to spell out the demands of love in concrete terms. For guilt implies a standard of judgment in terms of which moral conduct can be evaluated; it implies a structured order of moral relationships—of claims or demands—in terms of which moral choices can be measured. Viewed in punitive, legalistic terms, the experiences of guilt and judgment are spiritually destructive and dehumanizing; but,

47

understood in the context of grace and reconciliation, they point to the existence of a moral order that provides the possibility of meaning and integrity in ethical choices and human relationships. Recognition of man's responsibility for the evil consequences even of those actions which are motivated by goodwill is prerequisite for moral growth, for self-criticism, and for the reappraisal of moral conduct.

RULES, LAWS, AND PRINCIPLES

The central issue that Fletcher raises in *Situation Ethics* concerns the role of law in ethical reflection and decision-making. It has already been noted that for him situation ethics occupies a middle ground between antinomianism and legalism; thus Fletcher seeks to avoid the pitfalls of both of these alternative methods, but it is clear that he believes the real bête noire in ethics to be legalism. His polemic against legalism leads him to the very brink of antinomianism in the name of agape. Thus, in effect, he undercuts the "fruitful tension" which he recognizes between law and love in Christian ethics.[29]

According to Fletcher, one of the main strengths of situation ethics lies in its method of dialectical or polar analysis.[30] Unlike Christian moralists of the past, who tended to think in terms of either-or, situationists recognize three polarities in each ethical situation—law and love, authority and experience, and fixity and freedom. But the great weakness in Fletcher's method of ethical analysis is precisely his failure to preserve this dialectical tension between law and love and between fixity and freedom.

Fletcher is quite correct in assuming that for Christian

48

ethics there is only one unexceptional universal law or requirement; namely, agape. Hence he rejects all other universals of every kind.[31] But, when he does so, it is not clear just what kinds of norms are left, if any. For example, he seems on occasion to reject all principles except love; yet, in his desire to avoid the errors of such antinomians as the libertines, the "unprincipled" Gnostics, and the existentialists, he acknowledges the need for principles as "advisers without veto power."[32] Moreover, Fletcher is even more allergic to rules than he is to principles; and he is equally ambivalent in his attitude toward the former. On the one hand, he declares roundly, "For the situationist there are no rules—none at all"[33]; but, on the other hand, he recognizes that some rules may be necessary—even if they are only "rules of thumb."[34]

In his attack upon law—including rules and principles —Fletcher overlooks its disciplinary, educational, and neighbor-centered values. He assumes that ethicists who emphasize the importance of law for whatever reason— and, to a lesser extent, those who emphasize the role of principles and rules—always do so for the sake of the law itself rather than for the sake of the neighbor. He assumes that the only usage of law is prescriptive; hence, he ignores its illuminative role in helping the moral agent to understand the ethical situation itself instead of providing the latter with a prefabricated decision. Used in the service of love, law fills the need for direction in ethical reflection.

Fletcher's rejection of law is determined in part by his tendency to define the moral quality of an act exclusively in terms of its underlying motivation. If ethics were concerned only with motivation, without regard to the consequences of a choice, there would be no need for ethical directives. But Christian ethics is directed toward the meeting of the neighbor's needs, and love for the neighbor—not love of love—leads of necessity to consideration of the consequences of one's choices. And concern for the consequences of moral choices leads in turn to the need for law.

Although Fletcher rejects Reinhold Niebuhr's form of love perfectionism, he introduces another form of perfectionism when he writes, "The Christian ethic is not interested in reluctant virgins." [35] It is true that for Christian ethics the highest level of morality is that of love, where men and women are motivated by responsive love; but it is also true that among reluctant sinners law is also needed to provide discipline and guidance in the meeting of the objective needs of persons, whose good love intends and wills. If Fletcher's argument were carried to its logical conclusion, one would be forced to say that Christian ethics is not interested in reluctant non-murderers, reluctant non-thieves, reluctant participants in war, reluctant workers, or those who are reluctantly faithful to their marriage vows and family responsibilities; but in each of these instances Christian ethics is concerned about the meeting of the objective human needs even when people's hearts are hard.

CHRISTOLOGICAL OR MONOTHEISTIC ETHICS

Finally, Fletcher's situationist ethic raises the question of the uniqueness of Christian morality. According to him, the latter differs from all other forms of ethics only in regard to its underlying motivation. The special quality of Christian love is not found in the norm of love (agape) itself, for many non-Christians possess it and manifest it more fully than many Christians.[36] Rather, the uniqueness of Christian morality lies in its eucharistic quality and, more specifically, in its quality of thanksgiving to God for his love for mankind, which he has revealed most particularly in Christ. Christian ethics, in short, is not simply a theological ethic; it is essentially a christological ethic.[37] "The fact that the Christian ethic is theological gives it its species," but the fact "that it is christological gives it its particularity." [38]

Fletcher is doubtless correct in his insistence that the distinctiveness of Christian ethics is determined by the place which Jesus Christ occupies in Christian faith, for it is this which distinguishes the Christian ethic from that of Judaism and all other theological ethics. But, following Barth and Bonhoeffer, he tends to interpret Christian ethics too exclusively in christological and Christocentric terms. Moreover, he places the meaning of Christ too narrowly in the incarnation: "Take away the doctrine of the incarnation and the Christian ethic is nothing special whatsoever." [39]

In keeping with his Christocentrism, Fletcher interprets Christian morality almost entirely in terms of the New Testament. Theologically speaking, this is the basic weakness in his understanding of Christian ethics. The difficulty does not lie in what he affirms about the importance of Christology; it lies in his tendency to substitute christological analysis for theological analysis of man's ethical situation. He tends to interpret the New Testament message about God and man in isolation from that of the Old Testament. In reality, the two Testaments stand together as parts of a continuing disclosure of the divine will, and the New Testament cannot be properly understood except in the light of the Old Testament conception of God and his relationships to the world.

In the remainder of this chapter I shall attempt to describe in summary form an alternative interpretation of Christian ethics which provides a more adequate conception of man's moral existence and gives more attention to the nature and shape of responsibility in decision-making. In keeping with the purpose of this book, it is not possible to develop the implied position in a comprehensive and systematic form; hence, attention will be focused upon some of the major directions in which this approach to Christian ethics differs from that of Fletcher.[40]

SIMILARITIES TO FLETCHER

Although the focus of this description of an alternative conception of Christian ethics is upon differences between Fletcher's situationism and my own position, it should be recognized that the two interpretations of decision-making have many similarities. In the first place, both recognize the primacy of faith in moral reflection. For both, Christian ethics is theological ethics in that the former rests finally upon an underlying religious—or theological—conviction about the ultimate nature of that reality upon which the self is finally dependent. The conviction that that power which is sovereign throughout the universe is love is a gift of faith; and that conviction provides the basis, or starting point, upon which one who is grasped by that faith seeks to understand man's moral existence.

Second, Christian ethics is understood in each case in

terms of man's responsive love.[41] The Christian's love (agape) is a love that is called forth in the believer out of gratitude and thanksgiving to God for his love which has been made manifest to the community of faith. I believe, however, that Fletcher understands the divine action too exclusively in Christocentric terms.

Third, the two interpretations of Christian ethics begin at the same starting point: an effort to understand what is going on in man's moral experience. Both begin with an effort to understand the *is*ness, or givenness, of man's moral life, not with some abstract pattern (ideal) or ought (law) to which each new moral situation should conform. Both seek to understand the actual values and claims, the possibilities and duties, that are at stake in concrete moral decisions. For Fletcher, however, man's moral existence is largely unstructured; his emphasis is upon the uniqueness of each situation, upon the more individualistic and directly personal relationships of morality, and especially upon freedom. I believe that there is need for greater attention to the regularities, the constancies, and the structured character of moral relationships in order to give integrity and direction to moral choices.

In the fourth place, there is basic agreement between Fletcher's situationist ethic and my position because both are opposed to legalism and to antinomianism as these are generally understood in Christian ethics. The two interpretations differ, however, in regard to the importance which they attach to moral laws and principles in the process of decision-making. While rejecting a prescriptive use of law in an absolutist and literalistic sense, I see an indispensable place for law—including principles and rules—in ethical analysis. Law can serve as a source of illumination and guidance in the process of decision-making without being used prescriptively to produce prefabricated answers to ethical questions.[42]

Finally, both interpretations of Christian ethics rest upon a relational conception of value, of good and evil. In the language of H. Richard Niebuhr, value "has no existence in itself"; it is a function of "being in relation to being."[43] Thus, for Fletcher, love in human relations is a predicate term. But, whereas Fletcher tends to reduce all "virtues" to love, in my view the term virtue ("good" or "right") applies to any freely chosen action of moral beings that best meets the needs and potentialities of other beings to which and for which they are responsible.[44] Love is the inclusive and highest principle of Christian ethics, but it is dialectically—not substitutionally—related to other virtues such as justice and prudence.

METHOD OF DIALECTICAL (POLAR) ANALYSIS

According to Fletcher, situation ethics is more dialectical than traditional forms of morality in its understanding of decision-making. Compared with antinomianism (which rejects any role for law and the regularities of human existence) and legalism (which ignores the uniqueness of each moral choice), situationism seeks to preserve the polarity between law and love and between fixity and freedom. But Fletcher's conception of the dialectical method of analysis is far too limited, and he does not actually employ this method in dealing with the fundamental polarity with which the "new morality" is concerned, that of law and love.

In order to understand man's moral existence as a whole, including both the personal and group relationships of which it is composed, it is necessary to recognize a much larger number of polarities than the three to which Fletcher calls attention[45]; and it is necessary to maintain the tension in each polarity in a sharper and more consistent manner. The need for a more dialectical understanding of the relationship of love to law has been noted. In addition, the polarity between uniqueness and universality must be taken into account. The concept of particularity is itself incomprehensible apart from a generalized pattern of meaning. On the one hand, each moral situation is unique both because of the individuality of the persons involved in it and also because of the cultural and historical peculiarity of the context of each moral choice; yet, on the other hand, the very possibility of meaning in any moral situation depends upon its relatedness to a generalized pattern of values and/or duties in terms of which a single choice becomes intelligible. A proper comprehension of this polarity is prerequisite to understanding the relationship of freedom to law in Christian ethics.

Similarly, the antinomy between the claims of single individuals and those of the community is also present in every ethical situation involving more than two people. This antinomy is part of the given context in which love must do its work. While there is no final formula for determining how love will resolve the conflict between the competing claims of the individual and the group, it cannot do so responsibly unless the dialectical relationship between the two sets of claims is understood. Utilitarianism resolves this conflict too simply in terms of "the greatest good for the greatest number."

Not only is there an antinomy between the individual and the group, but often there is conflict among the various

55

needs and claims posed by a single individual or a single group. Thus there is need for love and for justice in the life of the community, and the latter cannot be reduced to the former without falsifying the antithetical as well as the complementary character of the relationship between these two values. When the relationships between justice and love are conceived in dialectical terms, the tension between them is maintained. Thus, justice is seen to be a necessary instrument—or structure or form—of love; but love is recognized to be the ultimate norm of justice so that all historical forms of justice stand under its final judgment.[46]

The same kinds of tensions and polarities which we have observed in man's moral experience are also present in his religious experience, and more particularly in his relationships to God and in the life of faith. Just as Christian ethics cannot be reduced to a monistic love ethic without doing violence to the complexities of the concrete moral situation, so the Christian conception of God cannot be reduced to Christology without obscuring the creative and ordering attributes of the divine will. In the development of a system of ethics or theology, the dialectical method of analysis provides a built-in safeguard against any form of reductionism which would negate or destroy the given dialectical relationships. I shall attempt to clarify the relationship between an essentially Trinitarian conception of Christian faith and the present interpretation of Christian ethics.

In biblical ethics as a whole, the understanding of God in terms of a threefold pattern of creation-judgment-salvation leads to a corresponding understanding of human life in terms of many needs and many duties. While the divine will for man cannot be reduced to codes of law, faith in the sovereignty of a righteous God leads to the necessary effort to understand the divine will in terms of its moral implications for man's life in culture. Ultimately this issue must be resolved by the believer in the concrete moral situation in the light of faith in the living God. Even so, the continuing qualities in man's response to God and to the neighbor are recognized in the Bible and described in terms of a number of symbols which help to clarify the meaning of the inclusive law of love. Among these biblical symbols are the concepts of commandment, law, obedience, covenant, righteousness, justice, mercy, loyalty, and faithfulness.

THE MEANING OF RESPONSIBILITY

The effort to understand the Christian life exclusively in terms of Christology and symbols drawn from the New Testament leads inevitably to a misunderstanding both of Christian faith and of Christian morality. Such an attempt is particularly disastrous insofar as the relationship of Christian faith to culture is concerned. Taken by itself, the New Testament does not provide the basis for an adequate understanding of God's purposive action in and through history; neither does it contain sufficient material for the development of a doctrine of creation, of social justice, or of man in relation to the natural world and human society as a whole.[47] In contrast to the New Testament, the Old Testament gives much greater attention to the sovereignty of God within history and contains a far more fully developed sense of man's social responsibility and his involvement in history and culture. These concepts are largely missing from Fletcher's interpretation of Christian ethics; and, because they are lacking, his "new morality" fails to provide an adequate basis for a viable social ethic. Even in

57

the area of more narrowly interpersonal relationships it is unable to do justice to the polarities—including those of law and love, uniqueness and universality, and love and justice—which are present in every ethical situation.

My analysis of the Christian life is based upon the conviction that the basic categories for understanding both Christian faith and Christian ethics are theological rather than christological. They are monotheistic and Trinitarian rather than Christocentric. The fundamental Christian belief about God is the belief that he is ultimately sovereign over the universe. On the basis of this conviction, Christian faith goes on to affirm that this sovereign God has revealed his will and his purpose for man in a climactic way in the events surrounding the incarnation, the life, the death, and the resurrection of Jesus. But the basic affirmation of the gospel is that the God who is known as Creator, as Judge, and as Redeemer in the Old Testament is the same God who was in Christ reconciling the world unto himself. That power which called all things into being has shown himself to be love.

Viewed in a Christian perspective, therefore, the ultimate context of every moral situation is that of the divine will; and that will is most fully understood in terms of the biblical conception of a unified but threefold universal pattern of creation, judgment, and reconciliation. This divine will provides the ultimate framework of meaning for every moral situation and all human decision-making. Of these concepts, that of creation is the most fundamental, and it is this which expresses the ultimate meaning and purpose of all finite existence, including cultural forms and structures, insofar as these are rooted in the nature of man as he is created. According to the biblical doctrine of creation, man was created free, but he was not given autonomy; on

58

the contrary, his essential humanity can be preserved and fulfilled only on the basis of his recognition and acceptance of the ordered pattern of creation—only through the acceptance of the orderly processes of nature, the givenness of the moral order, and his own finitude and dependence. Theologically, the Christian understanding of the meaning and significance of the structures of selfhood, of community (the "orders of creation"), and natural law (both physical and moral) is rooted in the doctrine of creation. This concept provides the basis for an understanding of the value and interrelatedness of the whole community of mankind and also for an understanding of the moral order—including justice, equality, freedom, love—upon which such a universal community must be built.

The biblical doctrine of creation provides the basis for dialogue between Christian ethics and the social sciences in a common effort to gain a fuller comprehension of the nature, the potentialities, and the needs of man. It provides the basis for cooperation with philosophy, with secular thought, and with other religions in an effort to gain a more adequate understanding of the meaning of human existence and the basic moral and theological issues with which all men, including the theologian, must wrestle. Without an adequate doctrine of creation, Christian ethics tends to be anti-cultural, individualistic, and socially irrelevant.[48]

Whereas the doctrine of creation emphasizes the positive value of the world of culture, the universality of the divine will, the oneness of the human community, and the final dependence of all finite beings upon the will and purpose of the Creator, the concept of God as judge, or orderer, emphasizes the continued sovereignty of the Creator over all that he has made and over all that he continues to call into being. The experience of judgment and "wrath" is also an inescapable part of the biblical apprehension of the divine will and presence, for man is related to God not only as the One who affirms his existence but also as the One who chastens him and judges him when he rebels against the Creator in pride and self-centeredness. The discernment of meaning in this judgment rests upon an ordered or structured pattern of comprehending the divine will in terms of which specific acts and decisions are recognized as sinful.

It was the prophets of the sixth to the eighth centuries B.C. who most fully apprehended the meaning of the sufferings and calamities which befell Israel in terms of the sovereignty of God and the divine judgments in history. They spoke in specific terms, for example, about the judgment of God upon the injustices and idolatries for which Israel was being punished—the giving of false weights and false measures, unequal justice, oppression of the poor, and unfaithfulness to the covenant which God had made with Israel. They broke through the hypocrisy of legalism and pious sentimentality and led Israel to a comprehension of her own concrete moral life in the ultimate context of her relationship to the Creator, whose will remained sovereign even when men rebelled against it.

According to the biblical understanding of human existence, man was created free, but God's judgments define the limits of that freedom; they point to the structures of freedom; thus they reveal the power and the righteousness of the Creator. Without an adequate apprehension of the judging and ordering pattern of the divine action in every moral situation, it is impossible to understand the full meaning of any particular moral choice, for "judgment" reveals the final seriousness of decision-making through the disclosure of the consequences of moral choices.

For the Christian, of course, the ultimate intention or purpose of the divine judgment is reconciliation or salvation; God's judgment is motivated by love. But when the concept of the divine love is divorced from that of the divine "wrath," the former easily becomes sentimentalized and immoral. Confrontation with the divine judgment reveals to man the deepest truth about himself and his communities—including nations—upon which that judgment falls. From the standpoint of Christian faith, the final purpose of such judgment is the fulfillment of the will of the Creator and the restoration of all men unto himself. In the words of Luther, the judgments of God are a "strange work" of love.

The final mode of divine action is that of reconciliation or salvation. It is this aspect of God's relationship to man that Fletcher emphasizes. However, because he tends to interpret the Christian doctrine of reconciliation too exclusively in terms of Christology and agape, he does not give adequate attention either to the relationships of salvation to creation and judgment or to the relationships between individual salvation and the transformation of culture. In the Old Testament, God is encountered as grace in the midst of man's cultural activity even while he is also met as the Judge who summons men to repentance and to social justice. While the ideas of creation and judgment are also present in the New Testament, in concepts such as the incarnation and the Last Judgment, the former tend to be developed in more individualistic terms in the New Testament due to the cultural situation in which the early Christians found themselves. Throughout the New

61

Testament period, for example, the Christians were without significant political and economic power to alter the prevailing social institutions; in addition, they expected the end of the present age to come in the relatively near future. Nevertheless, the Old Testament conceptions of the sovereignty of God in history and his lordship over culture are presupposed.

Like the morality of the prophets, Jesus' ethic is an ethic of "radical monotheism"; but the full meaning of that ethic cannot be understood in Christocentric or even christological terms. Like the prophets, Jesus pointed men beyond himself to God, to the God of Abraham, Isaac, and Jacob. He taught his followers to address this God as their heavenly Father; and he summoned them to radical obedience to him not out of fear as slaves to the law, but out of gratitude as faithful sons who delight to do their father's will. The God in whom Jesus taught his followers to put their trust, the God whom he summoned them to obey is sovereign over men and nations. Although Jesus summarized the whole duty of man in the twofold love commandment, he spoke of many other virtues even more frequently than he spoke of love; and he emphasized the abiding need for "the law and the prophets" to safeguard morality from hypocrisy and sentimentality.

A second major inadequacy in Fletcher's analysis centers in his concept of the nature of the self. Not only does Fletcher's christological interpretation of the context of decision-making need to be strengthened and corrected by placing it in the framework of a more universal pattern of theological meaning but also his concept of the self which decides and acts in the moral situation needs to be qualified by giving greater attention to the social and historical character of human existence. While it is

62

true that each individual must finally bear the responsibility for the moral choices which he is himself free to make and required to make, such decisions are made in companionship with many other selves upon whom each particular moral agent is dependent.

My interpretation of Christian ethics agrees with that of Fletcher in emphasizing both the existential quality of decision-making and the importance of taking into account the uniqueness of each moral situation. However, Fletcher conceives of the acting self in much too individualistic terms. The acting self must finally make its own moral choices, but it does not—and cannot—make them in isolation from many other selves which are its companions, its tutors, and its examples.[49] Biologically, intellectually, ethically, and psychologically, man is a social being who lives in community with his fellows. It is through his interactions with them that he comes to learn the meaning not only of selfhood but also of moral choices, of responsibility, and of good and evil.

The self, therefore, does not come to a particular moral situation as an isolated, solitary self. On the contrary, it comes with many concepts, many examples, and many experiences which it has assimilated and made its own; it comes with many tools of analysis which it employs, consciously and unconsciously, as it seeks to understand its relationships to other selves. In its decisions, which it makes in freedom and on the basis of its understanding of the good in the particular choice it alone can make, it is influenced by the patterns of meaning, of values and duties, which it has learned from other selves acting in similar situations. Without such a framework of meaning and interpretation, it would be impossible for the moral agent to comprehend the significance of each new choice.

This is true both of those relationships that are more narrowly personal and also of those which are more impersonal and inclusive—such, for example, as those involved in political and economic structures and in the community of nations. In all these situations the acting self exists in many relationships which it interprets in terms of patterns it has learned from other selves.

Meaning presupposes a structure or pattern of relationships, and the situation itself cannot be understood apart from such patterns and structures. Both from a biblical and from a sociological point of view, any attempt to comprehend the nature of the self apart from its interaction with other selves in community issues is an abstract conception of man and morality. Thus, Fletcher's failure to give adequate attention to the social dimensions of human existence leads him to neglect the social dimensions of morality as well as the structured character of human existence.

A third major inadequacy in Fletcher's analysis of the situation has already been suggested; namely, his tendency to view the self as making its moral decisions in an ahistorical present. Just as a moral agent always exists in a community of selves, so it also decides and acts in a present moment which is related both to the past through memory and to the future through anticipation. It is not just the acting self which comes to the moment of decision with a history that is remembered, but its response is also to other selves which are also present with their memories and expectations.

The self cannot understand its own identity as a social being apart from its memory of past experiences and past relationships, including past promises and commitments; and it cannot understand its ultimate worth apart from some projection of its past experience into the unknown future. Neither can any acting subject understand its neighbors—their needs, their patterns of behavior, their character, their probable responses to its own action toward them—apart from their history which is rooted in their past experiences and action. Knowledge of the past is prerequisite for interpreting the meaning in time, both for the present and the future, of human relationships.

More basically still, the moral agent who seeks to understand his moral existence from the standpoint of Christian faith inevitably does so in terms that include the historical past of the Christian community. The present-day believer inevitably wrestles with the meaning of the gospel in the light of his understanding of the witness of scripture and the church. In like manner, each believer is influenced in his apprehension of the meaning of Christ both for his personal moral conduct and for culture generally by his understanding of previous answers which have been given to these questions. The Christ of Christian faith is a historical Christ who is both remembered and expected. He is known in a historical community of faith in which his deeds are remembered and interpreted and in which also his teachings are remembered and proclaimed. Apart from the remembering of his deeds and the hearing of his message there would be no knowledge of this Christ, and no understanding of the meaning of obedience to him or of his lordship over the world.

In keeping with its greater historical awareness of the meaning of human existence, biblical ethics emphasizes the continuity and permanence of interpersonal and social relationships. In a fundamental sense, biblical ethics is covenant ethics—an ethic of remembering and being faithful to the covenant that God has made with Israel.

Truth-telling and promise-keeping are important, not because of the letter of the law but because of the neighbor's dependence upon the faithfulness and trustworthiness of the witness and the promiser. The permanence of the marriage bond is based not upon the continuance of emotional love, but upon faithfulness and loyalty to a bond that has been established through the joining together of man and woman in a "one-flesh union." [50]

Concepts such as these point to the historical quality of human existence, and they emphasize the importance of understanding human responsibility in terms that take into account man's inescapable involvement in time and history.[51] Similarly, the biblical conceptions of guilt and forgiveness express a historical understanding of human existence. For guilt is not something to be evaded or forgotten; rather, it is the wrong or evil quality of a moral or religious relationship—a quality to be acknowledged, repented of, and forgiven.

Because man is a being who lives in time and in history, his present needs and potentialities cannot be understood apart from his relationships to the past and the future. The full meaning of responsibility cannot be grasped, therefore, until these dimensions of human existence are taken into account.

4

The New Morality

*Does situation ethics do justice
to facts and faith?*

GABRIEL FACKRE

Newspaperman Tom Wolfe reports on a recent visit to
the planners of a popular television panel program:

> They showed me a big board with topics of prospective shows
> pinned up all over it. One of the topics was "Adultery—For or
> Against." One of the TV people told me, "We're having a problem
> with that one. We have some terrific people lined up to talk in
> favor of it. Norman Mailer and a lot of terrific people, but we
> haven't got anybody against!" [1]

The revolution in patterns of sex morality is too well
known to require documentation. The old codes are being
put into radical question by new theory and practice. An
umbrella term for the changing style is "the new morality." [2]

Gabriel Fackre is professor of theology and culture at Lancaster
Theological Seminary, Lancaster, Pennsylvania.

Squeezed under this covering idea is a variety of notions as to what newness means. Two major theses are au courant, one expounded by an articulate "secular" spokesman, and the other finding its protagonists in the "religious" community. The first can be called the *detached new morality* and the second, the *involved new morality*, or for shorthand purposes, the *cool* and *warm* moralities.

COOL MORALITY

Hugh Hefner, *Playboy* magazine, and the seventeen Playboy Clubs around the country are the prophet, scripture, and church of the detached new morality. As Harvey Cox points out in his perceptive *"Playboy's* Doctrine of Male,"[3] the picture of masculinity that comes through the magazine's stories, advice columns, photographs, advertisements, cartoons is that of a cool, casual character who knows how to mix a drink with finesse, has just the right stereo set, sports car, and necktie, and makes use of these accouterments with skill and detachment. The call to prayer he hears from the muezzin in the *Playboy* tower is, "Play it cool, man."

The cool posture applies, of course, to sex. Sex is for fun. It's good recreation. It's play. A real man needs his collection of "playmates"—in his monthly magazine foldout, and in real life. The worst thing that could happen to him is to get involved, entangled in the clutches of a woman who wants to tie him down with talk of love or marriage. Principal target of ridicule is the traditional code morality, which is portrayed as somber anti-sex and anti-joy.

In the cool play notion of sex, the girl emerges, as Cox observes, as a kind of accessory. The real man has his "in" cuff links, stereo, sports car, and playmate. Each is to be used as long as it is in style and doesn't get worn out. When no longer fun as a plaything, it may be disposed of. The girl is detachable like other items in the playboy's ensemble. It's no accident that the "bunny" has become the chief symbol of the cool morality.

WARM MORALITY

Sex is not something about which you can be detached. It is a matter of deep personal involvement. So affirms the warm new morality.

The condition for the sex act, according to proponents of the involved new morality, is the wholehearted commitment of two people to each other. Sex cannot be torn from love. The casual, nonchalant, recreational use of a woman is dehumanizing. Where there is a humanizing, caring relationship between two people, there sex finds its proper home.

This powerful critique of the thingifying of sex has been part of the long history of Christian reflection on the meaning of the relations between men and women. What, then, is new about this version of the new morality? Joseph Fletcher puts it this way:

> We cannot dogmatize. . . . Any sexual act (hetero-, homo-, auto-) engaged in, in or out of marriage, will sometimes be good and sometimes be bad, depending on the situation. . . . Sex for procreation or sex in marriage only is to me . . . warmed-over natural law. . . . The new morality would deny this and say rather that the right of any sexual act is to be determined by responsible calculation in the situation, not by prefabricated calculations.[4]

Or again:

> This neocasuistry repudiates any attempt to anticipate or prescribe real-life decisions in their existential particularity. . . . We

69

are always . . . commanded to act lovingly, but how to do it depends on our own *responsible* estimate of the situation. Only love is a constant; everything else is a variable. Is adultery wrong? . . . One can only respond, "I don't know. Maybe. Give me a case. Describe a real situation." [5]

Agape, understood as a "benevolence," which seeks the deepest welfare of particular persons in particular situations is the one absolute for this "situational" sex morality. One gets a fix on the polestar of love and looks afresh at each new occasion in the light of it. The mandates in the Christian memory that have to do with hetero-, homo-, and auto-sex behavior are, of course, in the background as "social wisdom" or "maxims," but one holds this "prefabricated" baggage lightly, being guided essentially by the decision-maker's careful assessment of the meaning of love in each context, by "responsible calculation in the situation."

SOME FACTS OF LIFE

Since the love-oriented involved morality is an inviting alternative to the code rigidities of the past and speaks persuasively of the humanizing of sex, let us begin our evaluation of the new morality with this warm version. And the beginning will be a very homely one.

Several years ago, my family and I launched an experiment in the doing of household chores. Husband and wife and five children reasoned: In this busy world in which there is such a varied traffic pattern in the home—after-school Girl Scouts, choir, athletic programs, meetings, and different arrival and departure times for work and school —we could not possibly keep a rigid schedule for table-setting, dishwashing, and cleaning responsibilities. The situation changed each day, and the situation of each person in the family was different. Why not then be fair about it and let each new day's context determine who does what? We became situationalists in our ethical theory. Let the doing of daily meal cleanup chores be determined by neighbor-love in each day's new context, a love which takes into account the needs and availability of each, seeking "the deepest welfare of particular persons in particular situations."

The experiment proceeded. Here is a typical slice of after-dinner conversation:

Mother: Well, Judy and Gay have to get ready for Girl Scouts and Bonnie says she has a big test in English tomorrow that she has to study for, so I guess Skye is the logical one to wash the dishes tonight.

Skye: Mommy, I washed them last night! How come I have to wash them again? That's not fair. Bonnie always gets out of the hard jobs by saying she has homework or something. I've got homework too!

Judy: Oh, Skye, stop whining. I got cheated all last week when you were sick in bed with a cold. Actually, you could have done more then, but you goofed off.

Skye: You be quiet! You haven't washed the dishes for three days. Besides you and Gay aren't going to Girl Scouts until 6:45 and you both would have plenty of time to wash them. You're just giving excuses!

Gay: We are not, Skye. We are supposed to be in charge of the program tonight and we have to get all the leather tools lined up and everything.

Mother: Bonnie, I just realized that you haven't washed the dishes now for a couple of weeks. Just when is your test?

Bonnie: Well, it's really not for two days, but it's a very hard test and I have to start now studying for it.

71

Mother: I thought you had it tomorrow! You can take fifteen minutes off and do the dishes. Skye has done them for the past two nights.

Bonnie: But, Mother, I just can't! Do you want me to flunk the test?

Mother: Well, you should have thought of that last night. You were downstairs watching "Hullabaloo" when you could have been studying.

Bonnie: Mom, I'm going to flunk that test and it will be your fault!

Father: Stop! I'll do the dishes.

Let me make a theological appraisal of what transpired. In seeking to operate with neighbor-love alone as a guide, certain things became apparent. To implement love in an open situation, there has to be objectivity in the assessment of the facts of the situation. Skye, for example, should be able to see that Judy and Gay did, in fact, have many preparations to make for the Scout program. Not being in their shoes, however, she was unable to see it. Mom, not sitting in Mrs. Musselman's English class as Bonnie does every day, could not possibly understand the heavy assignment that did in fact require two days' work. Everybody looks at a situation from his own vantage point. And because this is so, no one (except God himself) can see all the facts that are necessary to be seen in order to decide what love dictates in a given situation. This is the human condition that Christian theology has called "creatureliness," or finitude. We human beings are finite, limited creatures shaped by our peculiar past and present. Everything we see, therefore, is colored by this partial perspective, a fact which is driven home every time a group of witnesses positioned at different points on a street give conflicting reports of an accident. What we see is not "the situation," but *our version* of the situation.

There is another factor that extrudes itself in the process of living with the situation. Bonnie indeed could have given up the viewing of "Hullabaloo" the night before, knowing that she had an important test forthcoming, aware also that she had successfully avoided dishwashing for several weeks with her smallest sister Skye regularly absorbing the punishment of double duty. The fact is she chose to watch the TV program. Again, could not Gay and Judy have done their preparation that afternoon instead of waiting until the last minute? Also, it is interesting to observe the self-righteous fury of Dad. A closer look reveals that he had a burdensome writing deadline to meet that night, and was looking for a good excuse to postpone it, and at the same time throw up a pious smoke screen around his irresponsibility. In short, man's *personal interests* as well as his particular angle of vision enter into his definition of the situation in which he is counseled simply to mate love to fact. This, of course, is what Christian theology means by "sin." Its interesting subtleties are also evident in the way it expresses itself. No character in the little drama announces that he or she is selfishly asserting his own interests. No, each has a high-minded reason for the course of action taken—Bonnie is studying for a test, Gay and Judy have "Girl Scout duties," and Dad is "bringing peace to the household." Such piety neatly obscures the personal interests at stake and demonstrates why pharisaism is the most dangerous sin in the biblical catalog.

Eight months of the warm new morality in household affairs drove our family to a code of household conduct. On Mondays, "Judy, thou shalt do the chores"; on Tuesdays, "Bonnie, thou shalt do the chores"; and so on. To live out neighbor-love in the household situation, to assure some degree of justice to all, and to avoid the chaotic result of ignoring our finitude and sin, we bound ourselves to a set of rules.

Certainly there are exceptions. When Judy is sick on Monday, or Gay is at Girl Scout camp on Wednesday, the rules have to be set aside. There is a wise saying that there is an exception to every rule—and further, that the exception proves the rule. To acknowledge the fact of exception, however, is one thing. To erect that fact into an absolute which insists each situation is an exception allowing for no "prefabricated" rules, is quite another. In short, situationalism is a perfectly legitimate position if it is used itself situationally. This kind of *radical situationalism* applies its own judgment to itself: The theory cannot be made into an absolute, but is to be applied only in contexts where it is germane, and those contexts are the exceptions.

The great and good point made by the warm new morality is that human beings are the important thing in the Christian style of life. This is a telling blow against the detached posture of playboys. But the problem is not solved simply by affirming that neighbor-love is our absolute. The question remains: What in fact serves neighbor-love in sex relations? Does the assertion that one should get his heart in the right place first, and act responsibly in the situation, work to this end? Indeed it would, if men were wise enough and good enough to see all the facts in a given situation and act accordingly. Men, however, are not angels, with omniscience and purity. The *Time* magazine reporter commenting on Fletcher's entreaty not to be bound by "rules" but instead to seek out "in every decision-making moment" the neighbor's good observes, "Which is quite a long thought for an eighteen-year-old during a passionate moment in the back seat of a car." [6] This secular savvy neatly exposes the naïveté of moral counsel which ignores basic facts of the human condition.

The role of codes in Christian teaching is to do precisely what situationalists plead for—to make and keep life human, yet to do it in full awareness of the facts of finitude and sin. The biblical commandment "Thou shalt not kill" was hammered out in the covenant community because the God of the covenant honored human life. The mandate "Thou shalt not commit adultery" is also a judgment derived from the conviction that there is something so precious about the sex relationship that anything less than faithful love is dehumanizing. We shall return shortly to these positives after canvassing further the rationale for the negatives.

THE LEGISLATION OF MORALITY

In its rejection of codes, the warm morality makes some strange bedfellows. The belief that "love will find a way" without benefit of law (sometimes Augustine's declaration "Love God and do as you will" is inaccurately quoted in support of this),[7] is not unlike the refrain heard currently from segregationists and others seeking to resist social change: "You can't legislate morality." The pious plea that accompanies this dictum is: Forget the laws and confine yourself to the task of changing hearts.

It is true that one cannot make a bad man good by a new law.[8] But one can keep a good man safe. A traffic law is not going to convert a reckless, thoughtless driver into a considerate, humane one, but it may well deter him

75

from running someone down as his car screams to a halt before a red light. The point is that we Christians cannot wait until we convert all the reckless drivers into Christians. We need to set bounds to the chaos and injustice that irresponsible people can inflict on society—hence the need for laws. In the case of the struggle for Negro dignity, this means laws that will protect his elemental rights in voting, work, housing, and education from those who would deny them.

By the same token, moral law, as such, will not change a heart. Obviously we need more than legal mandate, particularly in Christian faith, which declares we are not saved by law but by grace. While law will not save, a generation that is nourished in respect for its wisdom will have some standards to keep its impulses in check. When we take as seriously the need to set boundaries to our self-love in personal sex morality as we do in public civil rights, the utopian assumption that all that is needed is to get one's heart in the right place is properly exposed. Law is not the enemy of love. It is the expression of it. This is as true in sex rights as it is in civil rights.

JESUS, PAUL, AND THE LAW

A favorite text of the warm morality is Mark 2:23-28— Christ's breach of a rigid interpretation of sabbath law, and his explanation of the action, "The sabbath was made for man, not man for the sabbath." Does not freedom in Christ mean this kind of freedom from the law for us as well?

There is a wealth of meaning in this passage. Ironically, its central intent may well be precisely the opposite of the interpretation given to it by the situationalist. The mechanical observance of the sabbath requirement, and the heavy barnacles of interpretation that grew up around it, had virtually obscured the central motif of the fourth commandment. The letter had killed the spirit. How does one shake people out of this mesmerism of the minutia? Christ opted for a demonstration in the grainfields in which the intent of the law was dramatized at the expense of attention to its details. The point made was that this ritual observance had a human meaning. It was on the books *for man:* the sabbath was made for man. Or putting it another way, love is the ground and goal of the law; Christ is Lord of the sabbath.

As well as pointing to the humanizing source of the law, this passage is an affirmation that rote observance of the letter, or its casuistic refinement, are not enough, for we Christians are called to commitment to the Love that is the ground and Lord of the law. And, further, it means that the motif of sabbath rest must be brought under the critical scrutiny of its source to assure that its going usage is indeed *for man.* In short, Christ is the fulfillment not the negation of the law. In the encounters with the rich young man and the adulteress, Christ does not disregard but presupposes law. The full power of his compassion is brought home in the latter case precisely because he takes adultery seriously, yet finds it in his heart to accept the unacceptable.

What then of Paul's insistence that we are not saved by the law, but by faith? Yes, this is a central theme of the gospel. To transcend law, however, is not to dissolve it, any more than the presence of the New Testament abolishes the significance of the Old. (There is an interesting correlation between the Marcionite rejection of the Old Testament and its lawgiver God in favor of a properly expur-

77

gated New Testament with its God of love, and the zeal to replace law by love in ethical theory.) Paul's declaration that the law is "holy, just, and good" is intimately related to his bout with it. Out of his own profound struggle to live up to the law (vis-à-vis the commandment against covetousness, for example, Romans 7:7-25), as that law was animated, internalized, and radicalized in love by the Lord of the law, Jesus Christ, he was driven to his knees in penitence. In that confrontation the word of divine mercy and the meaning of grace was born for him. Hence, law for Paul is a "schoolmaster" preparing us for the coming of grace, and in our half-and-half Christian life, *simul justus et peccator*, serving as a continuing guideline.

Law is a fundamental theme in the teaching of Christ and Paul. To understand its penultimate role in the life of faith is no mean task, the difficulty of which is amply demonstrated by the constant appearance in Christian history of legalisms which seek to elevate it to ultimate significance as the way of salvation, on the one hand, and antinomianisms on the other, which eliminate it altogether on the grounds that faith and/or love render it unnecessary.

CODE, CREED, AND COMMUNITY

That no man is an island is a familiar note in both contemporary theology and sociology. Man is born, nourished, and becomes a man in the network of interrelations that make up the human community. So too, man is born, nourished, and becomes a man of faith in the supportive fabric of the faith community. The Christian faith community, in particular, speaks of the marriage of Christ to the church and disavows any individualistic claim that the Christian life can be fully authentic in abstraction from the Christian life together.

One expression of sensitivity to the corporate note is the use in Christian history of shared testimonies of faith. A "creed" is the fruit of communal reflection on the meaning of faith. To recognize the value of the classic confessions of faith, such as the Apostles' and Nicene Creeds, and the continuing need for the church to hone new statements of faith relevant to a changing world, is to affirm that a Christian cannot simply write his own religious ticket. As a member of a larger community of Christians, he is a partner in its heritage and its continuing struggle to bear a shared witness to its times. He does not operate "by his lonesome," developing his own version of Christianity in lordly isolation from the brethren.

A code, like a creed, is the product of the covenant community's reflection on its mandate. To take the communal dimension of Christian faith seriously in the sphere of morality is to respect the research the community has done, is doing, or ought to do, in that sphere as well as in the area of Christian doctrine. Where there has been a research consensus that points to code guidelines in sex morality, a Christian committed to a communal view of faith will not lightly dismiss them. A "play-it-by-ear" morality that speaks of love finding its own way in each situation is really the same kind of rugged individualism in morality as the rejection of testimonies of faith is in the area of doctrine. Neither takes seriously the organismic nature of Christian faith.

The need for developing new codes is as manifest as that of the need for restatements of faith. Where fantastic new moral questions surface, ones for which there is no fund of communal wisdom (such as the issues of prenatal genetic control, the creation of life in the laboratory, and the possibilities of the indefinite extension of human life with its attendant questions of "death management" and the like), the church has a responsibility to muster its reflective resources and develop guidelines for decision-making in these areas. No man, including church-man, is an island that can afford to neglect the insights of either the mainland of the human community or the faith community.

GOD'S KNOWING AND OURS

Up to this point we have dwelt on the negatives—the need for guidelines in sex morality necessitated by the facts of creatureliness, sin, and community, and in faithfulness to the biblical teaching about law itself. The presence of a firm "no" has its roots ultimately in the biblical "yes" to sex. The fact that sex is precious, lovely—yes, fun!—is the positive at the heart of the matter.

"A man leaves his father and his mother and cleaves to his wife, and they became one flesh. And the man and his wife were both naked, and were not ashamed." That is not from *Never on Sunday* but from the Bible—Genesis 2:24-25. This frank and exuberant report is echoed in the biblical description of the sex act: "Adam knew Eve. . . . Cain knew his wife. . . . Elkanah knew Hannah." Sex is *knowing* another person. The mystery of the other's being is disclosed. The two are no longer separate, but are "one flesh." In the coming together of a man and a woman the secret of the universe is let out. The alienation that is everywhere apparent is challenged by the oneness here embodied. Mystics talk about knowing God in contemplative ecstasy, but the Bible speaks of knowing in the sex relationship. The Bible is an earthy document that speaks about an earthy God—creator of matter, enfleshed in Jesus, present now in the solidities of history and its institutions, and ultimately transfigurer of it—who is the farthest thing from the hazy spirituality of present or past gnostics. God is for man, and this means, in the present context, for sex.

The seriousness with which the Bible takes sex is manifest in commentary on its indelibility and the wound it leaves theologically when it is abused. Paul says, "Do you not know that he who joins himself to a prostitute becomes one body with her? For, as it is written, 'The two shall become one'" (1 Cor. 6:16).

Another thing comes clear in the biblical understanding of the one-flesh union. It is a jealous relationship, taking place between just two people. We do not hear about Adam and Eve and Jane, or Adam and Sam and Eve. Sex is a closed corporation. How is it possible to have this deep personal knowing passed around? The parallel here to the relationship with deity is striking. God does not tolerate competition. Separated by only a few lines are the declarations "The Lord your God is a jealous God" and "Thou shalt not commit adultery." In fact the Old Testament speaks of a person or nation faithless to God as one that goes "awhoring after other gods."

God seals the singular relation between his chosen people and himself with covenant vows. So, too, the one-to-one bond between a man and a woman is made firm in the covenant of marriage. As God's unconditional, steadfast love is promised through thick and thin, so the wedding vows mirror this in-spite-of love which persists through sorrow as well as joy, sickness as well as health, want as well as plenty. Again it is no accident that the marriage service begins with the moving words "Compared by St. Paul to the mystical union between Christ and his church," for the union between husband and wife is a broken reflection of the divine action itself. As Roger Mehl says:

> If scripture accords to marriage, among all other human institutions, an exclusive privilege, if it compares the love of a man for his wife to the love of Christ for his church, it is because it well perceives that mysterious bond between conjugal union and the kingdom, the prefiguration of reconciliation and the final recapitulation in this very humble, very banal, and very impure encounter of a man and a woman.[9]

CREATION AND PROCREATION

God is Redeemer and he is Creator. He knows man and he makes man. Marriage is a mirror of God's redemptive I-Thou love, and his creative love as well. The covenant union between two people is for knowing, and also for making. God is Creator. Man is procreator.

The Roman Catholic Church has long insisted that the basic reason for marriage is procreation. Its misgivings about birth control follow naturally. However, in the ferment of renewal current in the Roman communion there is being heard a growing plea to consider the profound significance of conjugal togetherness—one flesh knowing —as a companion purpose. If this receives formal endorsement, a reconsideration of the birth control position may eventuate.

Do we Protestant Christians have something to learn here from our Roman Catholic friends? If they are beginning to see the conjugal love dimension of sex—a point made strongly by Protestant Christianity—we ought to take a second look at their firm commitment to the bearing of children as a fundamental purpose of marriage.

Protestant Christians have always acknowledged the importance of the biblical injunction to "be fruitful and multiply." To take it with greater seriousness, as is urged by Paul Ramsey, is to shed considerable light on both the moralities of detachment and involvement. For one, any detached sex relation to another, embarked upon as simply a natural extension of the handshake, or for the gratification that goes with the use of a plaything, is a clear abuse of the purpose which includes responsible bringing of new life into the world. For another, to use the gift of procreation in a sexual relation outside of marriage on the grounds that it is a humanizing act of neighbor-love is as faithless to the procreative purpose of marriage as is the morality of detachment. The humanizing, neighbor-loving expression of sex *includes* the responsible bringing of life into the world, and its nurture in the bosom of a family (not in every sex act, of course, but as an intrinsic part of the total relationship of two persons in marital covenant). Whether sex is engaged in outside of marriage "for kicks" or "because we love each other," it plays havoc with the divine intent for a man and a woman to beget and take responsibility for the fruit of the womb.

Marriage in its creating as well as its redeeming dimension is a mirror of the life of God himself. His creativity and divine love are, for Christian eyes, reflected in the procreativity and human love of a man and a woman sealed together in the marriage bond.

INSIGHTS OF THE NEW MORALITY

While we have dwelt here on the shortcomings of the new morality, cool and warm, implicit in this critique is an appreciation for the genuine biblical themes which are underscored by both in the face of their neglect by overeager defenders of the old morality (the "hatpin brigade," as Hefner calls them). One such insight is the note of joy in the facts and processes of the created order, specifically the sex facts and processes. A somber puritanism is rightly criticized by all forms of the new morality, for it is more gnostic and docetic than Christian.

Another genuinely important accent of the involved new morality is its reminder of the "for man" style of the Christian faith. On the one hand, in its plea for persons it has helped to shape the indictment of the dehumanizing sex represented by the cool morality and all forms of human exploitation at work in the current "sexplosion." On the other hand, it has properly rebuked the thoughtless rote observance of law, and the authoritarian defense of it resorted to so frequently by proponents of the old morality. A healthy response to that attack is not blind defense of codes, but a serious look at their purpose and a consequent interpretation of the "for man" intent that lies behind the sex disciplines of the Christian community.

The corollary of a "for man" thrust is the willingness to scrutinize all the moral baggage of the church, and all the new issues, in the light of the neighbor-love mandate. This will mean the restatement of inherited notions that have had a relevance in another day but no longer are instruments of neighbor-love. It will mean the development of guidelines for new kinds of decision-making pressed upon us by new moral issues for which there is no fund of research in the Christian treasury. And it will also reinforce our awareness that the higher law of love may require an exception to the very rules that are the normal structures of that love.

84

The new morality is a sign of, and a serious attempt to come to terms with, the fact of modern secularization. As secularization lifts up the importance of this-worldly, human terrain and puts into question religious authority figures, so the new morality in both its forms affirms man's coming-of-age, his right to have his voice and experience heard in matters of sex, his right to be more than a submissive child who is told by traditional religion what to do and what not to do.

How can faith rightly celebrate man's coming-of-age and yet do it without capitulating to the new morality's naïveté about the wisdom and virtue of an ageric age? Perhaps the developmental process in human life gives us a clue. The adolescence of the race, like the adolescent stage in personal growth, is a time of rebellion against old authorities, a pressing forward out of the period of dependency. To demand uncritical submission to the orders of aged authorities, human or divine, is to retard development and cripple an emerging humanity. God wills maturity. He wants a man to be a man. Yet adolescence is not adulthood. True maturity comes when the son has secured his identity and, no longer in need of revolt, establishes a new relationship with the father, a partnership of free selves who listen to, and affirm, each other simply for who they are. The monologues of both authority and rebellion pass into authentic dialogue. Thus Christian morality comes of age when it ceases to demand uncritical obeisance, when it offers itself as a servant rather than as a master, as a resource rather than source, when it seeks to give reasons why it believes its perspective illumines the human scene, and when it in turn listens for what it might learn from the new man about the new day. The other partner in the dialogue also comes of age when, free of the need to establish his identity by revolt, he can ask what "the fathers" might have to share with "the sons."

Another dissatisfaction properly aimed at the old morality, one inadequately developed by either version of the new morality we have here discussed, is its "angelism." A moral stance consisting simply of a plea to live up to the codes, or for that matter to live out "benevolence," which does not at the same time take into account the creaturely setting of the person who is so addressed (for example, his or her embeddedness in a Negro ghetto where the normal family patterns are shattered by the long-standing scar of slave days, and where the desperation of slum-living and discrimination easily precipitate those not far advanced in saintliness into frenzied escape routes, the most convenient being promiscuous sex) is an unbiblical notion which assumes that man is a disembodied spirit, detached angel-like from the vicissitudes of his physical-social rootage. While no man is a complete captive to his environment, loud moral exhortation is not the answer. On the basis of the doctrine of man as enfleshed spirit, Christian faith recognizes that the plight of the oppressed and disadvantaged cannot be overcome by pleading with them to pull themselves up by their bootstraps. We challenge the voting, housing, work, and educational patterns that are the springboards to their demoralization. The same is true of those who abuse the gift of sex. From mass media that commercialize and exploit sex to the ghetto despair which propels its victims into the anodyne of promiscuity, the structures of society are indeed part of the question of sex morality. Any version of old or new morality which feels its job is done by finger-wagging entreaties is talking in the air to disembodied angels, not flesh and blood

86

men, and consequently is irrelevant to the problems of human conduct.

BEYOND THE OLD AND NEW MORALITIES

"Neither . . . circumcision nor uncircumcision, . . . but Christ" (Col. 3:11, KJV). The man in Christ is a free man chained neither to the old legalisms nor to the latest "in" styles of thought and practice. He is free enough to believe in an open future, full of unresolved questions, free also to choose the yoke of discipline of the Body of which he is an organic part, a community whose research and wisdom he honors. He is not captive to the loveless code of the legalist. But he is free as well from the codeless love of the new morality, which has not adequately measured the depths of the human problem of creatureliness, sin, and individualism, nor the heights of knowing and making. True freedom is the way of faithful love, a love that finds its embodiment in a joyful, responsible, caring, sharing union—the one flesh mystery of a man and a woman in lifelong covenant.

5

When Love Becomes Excarnate

How does one know *he is*
serving love in the situation?

HARMON L. SMITH

Whether one *knows* that he is or is not serving love in a
given situation is, in the first instance, an epistemological
problem, not an ethical problem. For what is at stake, at
least initially, is not a moral judgment about either be-
havioral models or specific moments of conduct but a
critical understanding of agape and the viability for its
expression in a given situation.

The meaning of love, Christianly understood, and
whether it is in any sense a possibility for human, personal existence has long provoked profound and polemical
discussions in theology and ethics. Indeed, from one perspective the history of Christian thought can be interpreted as the continuing effort to state an appropriate re-

Harmon L. Smith is assistant professor of Christian ethics at Duke
University Divinity School, Durham, North Carolina.

lationship between divine grace and human moral agency. If the error of one generation is its extravagant claim for man's freedom in such a way as effectively to denigrate God's sovereignty, the mistake of the next will likely be just the converse. This observation alone is probably enough warrant for the assumption that a definitive theology or ethics in terms of one or another alternative will continue to elude us, both linguistically and conceptually. A more or less adequate understanding will then have to be one that faithfully embraces both freedom and sovereignty and holds them in dialectical tension, distinguishing but not separating. In this way it may be possible, for example, to claim with some measure of integrity and discernment that man is simultaneously a self-determining moral agent and a creature dependent upon the assistance of divine grace. Failure to acknowledge this bifocal character of theological ethics is the rock upon which all theological and ethical systems inevitably founder.

In the face of burgeoning secular humanisms, which stress the autonomy of ethics, no more urgent question confronts the contemporary ethicist than whether he can seriously entertain any meaningful correspondence between God's intention for the world and his activity in it, and the conduct of persons. The thesis of this essay is that the moral implications of Christian theism insist upon an affirmative answer to that question and that the doctrines of incarnation and justification by grace alone best suggest how that answer is to be formulated and articulated.

There are currently three somewhat distinct ways of doing Christian ethics, each competing for professional and popular acceptance. Each has historical antecedents, demonstrating again that there is nothing entirely new under the sun; but I am concerned here chiefly with contemporary models. These ways may conveniently be called legalism, extemporism, and situationism. All three share in common, despite methodological differences, a tendency to drive an irreducible wedge between God's love and the possibility of its expression in man's actions.

At the outset, it ought to be said that one criterion for assessing the validity and functional utility of these alternative ethical positions will be whether any or all of them adequately deal with the reality of *creative risk* in decision-making. Where a position fails adequately to deal with this risk, which I think lies at the heart of decision-making (as well as in the consequences of a decision made), there is reason to suspect that the standpoint is deficient both humanly and theologically.

Another assumption that informs the development of this essay should be made explicit: If both legalism and extemporism are found to be inadequate in a fundamental way for the expression of the human act of decision-making, that is, in overlooking creative risk *within* the decision-making process itself, nothing can be gained toward a basically different direction by trying (as situationism expressly does) to walk between them, because such a walk takes its direction if not its steps from the same presuppositions that shape legalism and extemporism. In other words, if another genuine alternative is possible, it must be a radical one: It must start by reconstituting the ground upon which the ethical system is built. To use an agricultural metaphor, we need to dig up and plow, rather than merely harrow together.

The full establishment of my case, particularly as regards legalism and extemporism, requires more complete

90

argumentation than space permits. Nevertheless, and at the risk of misrepresentation, both these approaches deserve attention, however brief and insufficient.

LEGALISM

The legalist approaches decision-making with the assumption that there is a standard of conduct, explicitly formulated in terms of enjoined and prohibited actions, which must be applied to every person, in every situation, in exactly the same way. Whether these injunctions derive from natural law, as Roman Catholic moralists argue, or from biblical literalism, as Protestant conservatives claim, they have unconditional validity as *given* demands that an individual accepts or rejects but does not modify. These demands are given because they are presumed to be "revelatory definitions of the nature of agape," [1] and are in no way dependent upon man's developed moral sense. They are supposed to be objectively and eternally valid and remain unchanged amid relativity and flux.

In this view, the "right" and the "good" tend to become synonymous with the "correct," as it is defined by reference to some normative framework for the conduct of human affairs which has been directly and unequivocally communicated as the will of God. A person thus *knows* that he is showing love in a situation if he is being obedient to a command explicitly directed to that situation. Love, legalistically understood, is not so much an attitude or relational category as it is an axiomatic description of correct and proper human behavior.

Criticisms of this position are chiefly of two types. First, legalism is vulnerable to the judgment that if man is in possession of an eternally valid body of moral laws, the living presence of God is both unnecessary and effectively denied. God becomes superfluous as living reality in the measure to which his intention is made coterminous with some historically given command of fixed content. To absolutize moral maxims is, ipso facto, to foreclose both the need for and the possibility of God's continuing communication of himself. Second, the unbending insistence that there are some acts everywhere and always right, and others correspondingly wrong, fails to appreciate the uniqueness of each historical moment. Legalism, then, tends to be both irresponsible to God's present reality and irrelevant to the particularities of human existence.[2]

EXTEMPORISM

Because it has never enjoyed serious advocacy by large numbers of Christians, the extemporist approach is less pertinent to the present debate; nonetheless it is worth brief mention, if only to state the supposed alternative to legalism. The classical Protestant example of extemporism is John Agricola of Eisleben, a contemporary of Luther's, who vigorously insisted upon free and unconditional grace and liberty from every form of law. Probably more familiar, however, is the theology of the Inner Light as advocated by men like Thomas Muenzer, Caspar Schwenkfeld, George Fox, and William Penn.

The critical feature of this teaching, for present purposes, is its radical subjectivism and individualism. All men, according to this doctrine, have been endowed with the principle of an inner light by which they may distinguish good and evil and through which they may receive direct communication from God. In consequence, all externalized and objectified revelation (such as the Bible) must be regarded as subordinate to the unmediated illumination of the inner light, which alone is the clear and unmistakable communication of God to the self. No positive law, not even biblical injunction, is acknowledged to have precedence over that divine "something" that slumbers in the recesses of the human "soul." Certain forms of Protestant and Roman Catholic piety still affirm this position, although adherents to both varieties are relatively few in number. Usually the contemporary extemporist is of a more or less existentialist stamp, and better called an extemporist than an antinomian.[3]

In contrast to the legalist, who treats his life as though it were a fabric in which each thread of experience has by divine command its distinct and unambiguous place, the extemporist acknowledges no connection between the several threads of his experience. Each is so unique as to be discontinuous with all others. If life is to be characterized by anything, it is absurdity, not purpose. There is no way for the extemporist to formulate guides or principles for the conduct of life because his existence is so profoundly fragmented that generalizations about it are impossible. Consequently, his decisions and actions appear spontaneous, irregular, incoherent, and unprincipled.

Given this circumstance, the question "How does one know that he is serving love in the situation?" is obviously misplaced and irrelevant. "Love," for the extemporist, is ephemeral, evocative, emotive, a nonlogical category; as such, it is empty and meaningless, defined by a nonsensical juxtaposition of words. In this process, "knowing" becomes a category of immediacy, not reflection, and it is reduced to the wholly psychic and subjective level of

93

feeling. As an unconditioned and arbitrary response to unrelated stimuli, the knowing process is thus constituted ex nihilo. Epistemologically as well as ontologically, the extemporist affirms a radical discontinuity between existential moments, thus asserting the fundamental incoherence of reality. For him the real is the self spontaneously and reflexively responding to its immediate environment; but this environment is one that the self creates because any other kind is presumed to be valueless. In sum, the creative act is the value-creator.

God, or whatever might be represented by that word, is therefore superfluous for the extemporist. At bottom, the self has become "god," and selfishness, even though it may express itself in noble and humanitarian activity, is its own informing moral precommitment. As with the legalist, what the extemporist calls love is only a form of egoism; his participation in situations with neighbors is as one who stands over against them, who may be momentarily but not lastingly affected by mutual involvement, and who therefore does not give himself in the decisive and actual moment of their encounter.

This relationship (if it can be called that) is an excarnation; that is, a disembodiment or depersonalization of love in the measure to which the self does not genuinely embrace the neighbor as a living embodiment of the self's affection. Bereft of more coherent and stable resources than his own capriciousness, the extemporist has no choice but to seek the improvement of life's problems in modes of thought which lead logically toward either a skepticism that sees little significance in the moral struggle—nihilism—or to a complete secularization of life in which all norms disintegrate in relativity, and expediency is the only wisdom.

94

SITUATIONISM

The third of the major alternatives currently present-
ing themselves as theoretical models for decision-making
is variously described as situationism or contextualism.
This way of doing ethics is more or less the product of
both legalism and existentialism and, accordingly, offers
itself as a via media between the two extremes. Because
of its vogue, but more importantly because it represents
a serious challenge to traditional approaches, it is necessary to examine it more thoroughly than the other two.
Joseph Fletcher's *Situation Ethics,* in this regard, deserves
special attention because it is the most cogent and coherent argument for situationism yet to appear in print.

Instead of asking the legal question "What ought I to
do?" or the extempore question "What am I to do?" the
situationist poses as the first question in ethics "What do
I want?" [4] The primary problem is thus one of values, the
choice of one's summum bonum. By casting the ethical
question this way, Fletcher intends that situation ethics
be relieved of the burden of inviolable rules that have to
be applied always and to everybody alike, and yet not
entirely void of guides and thus wholly reliant upon the
situation to offer its own solution. Situation ethics thus
enters the decision-making context armed with principles,
but they are hypothetical not categorical; they are not to
be treated as inviolable laws but depend for validity upon
their applicability in a situation. These principles may be
either compromised or completely abandoned, "if love
seems better served by doing so." [5]

To the question "What guides decisions when principles are abandoned?" Fletcher answers:

Christian situation ethics has only one norm or principle or law
. . . that is binding and unexceptionable, always good and right
regardless of the circumstances. That is "love"—the agape of the
summary commandment to love God and the neighbor. Everything else . . . [is] only *contingent,* only valid *if they happen* to
serve love in any situation.[6]

This, in sum, is the substance of the position taken by
situationism; and Fletcher has probably argued the case
as convincingly as anyone (in our situation) can. This is
not to say, however, that the case is convincing. At least
certain questions deserve to be raised, and an observation
or two may then be in order.

In the first place, it is not at all certain that the way of
situation ethics really offers a via media. Its emphasis is
plainly on teleology, and a role for deontological ethics is
at best ambiguous. The only acknowledged imperative
merely enjoins one to will whatever in the situation may
be right; but what is right is calculated in terms of a
summum bonum that "is neighbor-centered first and
last."[7] This statement, however, is mistaken if one recalls
that historically the summum bonum in Christian thought
has typically been seen as integral to the *summum esse;*
and that, therefore, to ask the question of the highest
good is to speak within both ontological and hierarchical
categories. Yet Fletcher maintains that the neighbor's
good cannot be anticipatorily prescribed by reference to
any such esse; in the words of Bonhoeffer, it can only be
decided in each "definite, yet unconcluded, unique and
transient situation."[8] The reason for this may be understood, provisionally perhaps, by taking a closer look at
Fletcher's understanding and use of agape.

What guides a person in willing the neighbor's good
in the situation is, of course, love. But this is love regarded

as a predicate only; that is, as nonsubstantive and formal, as a principle that expresses "what type of real actions Christians are to call good." [9] Agape, Fletcher argues, is nothing "given" or objectively real or self-existent in the context of our existence. He writes:

> Only in the divine being, only in God, is love substantive. With men it is a formal principle, a predicate. Only with God is it a property. This is because God *is* love. Men, who are finite, only *do* love.[10]

In so stating his case, Fletcher has opted for a transcendent form in the classical Platonic tradition and, having allowed the rules of the game to be thus set, he is beaten before play begins—unless he can devise some strategy by which the "real" can be experienced and evaluated without reference to the "ideal." But this is highly unlikely with the way he has chosen.

He has so defined "situation" as to make it ready-made, a simple "that's how it is," just as Platonic thought defined the being of man as ready-made. What was nonbeing to Plato—the world of becoming—is simple being for Fletcher; and Fletcher's nonbeing (that which cannot be structured) is consciousness. This is basically an ahistorical approach because it depends upon excarnate ways of thinking about being and value. There is here no intrinsic communion between being and nonbeing, or between the decision-maker and the situation in which he has to make decisions. For Fletcher, one is not embodied in a situation; he is simply "up against" a situation; what one does *in* the situation has no serious corollary to what the person becomes. The irony of this situational approach is that it is thoroughly nonsituational! The situation, as "objective circumstances," [11] is alien to everything about

97

it and everyone involved in it; it is simply "the case" or "what is."

Love, however, cannot be taken arbitrarily or placed outside the world and then brought back via situational problematics. If agape is not somehow "given" in the context of our existence, our situation must always be regarded as extrinsic to agape; if this be the case, then the problem of the "good" can never arise because agape cannot become embodied in acts in which the person, his situation, and his decision are inseparable factors affecting one another. Just the antithesis of this view, though, is the summary of the gospel in 1 John 4:19: The very possibility of our love is grounded in the reality of God's having first loved us.

Whatever else Fletcher's understanding and use of agape may mean, it certainly suggests that agape is not a human possibility on any terms and that therefore we do not, in any serious sense, genuinely participate in the redemptive love of God. The command "to be like God, to imitate him," [12] is thus meaningless owing to man's incapacity for the love of which only God is capable; and our decisions and actions are thereby limited to a kind of heroic fatalism.

Urgent questions are raised in this context about the reality and bearing of incarnation upon the doing of situational ethics. Christian ethics has traditionally held not only that the *imitatio Dei* is a distinct possibility for one who acknowledges that God was in Christ but also that obedience to that prototypal divine love manifested in him is explicitly commanded. To be sure, Fletcher refers to Christ; but this occurs chiefly in support of the situationist's opposition to legalism. The other side of the coin is quite neglected; namely, that Jesus positively enjoins his disciples to fulfill certain concrete responsibilities; for example, to love the neighbor as oneself. And the apostle Paul follows this prescription, admonishing his readers to "have this mind among yourselves, which you have in Christ Jesus" and "bear one another's burdens," and reminding them that love neither serves itself nor has its own way.

If we are incapable of expressing agape particularly and concretely, then we need to be shown how this is so in view of the incarnation, which confronts us with both our tragedy and our destiny. Meanwhile, it is a more tenable position that love, like consciousness, is always incarnate; it is a being-in-the-world through my being-in-my-body, a being that is fluid without being groundless, structured and structuring without being substantive and forever the same.[13] When *Situation Ethics* speaks of agape, however, it is excarnate and for that reason nonsituational.

In this connection, we should recall that situationism asserts love to be a principle that expresses "what type of real actions Christians are to call good." Fletcher points out that these actions, as indicative of value, are worthy only because the action "happens to help persons (thus being good) or to hurt persons (thus being bad)."[14] He argues further:

Apart from the helping or hurting of people, ethical judgments or evaluations are meaningless. . . . Christian situation ethics asserts firmly and definitely: *Value, worth, ethical quality, goodness or badness, right or wrong—these things are only predicates, they are not properties.*[15]

In other words, situation ethics is nominalistic, but with a twist: Whereas medievalists argued that good is good because God wills it, Fletcher argues that man makes this decision. Objective value theory, in whatever guise, is summarily rejected.

But how does a person know that he is doing (or has done) the loving thing in the situation? What judges decision and action? Given the situationist's description of love and his use of principles as illuminators but not directors, one wonders whether in this sense they retain whatever it is that denominates them "principles" in the first place. Situation ethics "does not ask *what* is good but *how* to do good for *whom;* not what *is* love but how to *do* the most loving thing possible in the situation." [16] This mark of existentialism, the reduction of the criteria for moral judgment to sincerity and integrity, "while supremely relevant in assessing praiseworthiness and blameworthiness," as G. F. Woods says, "does not provide any clear ground for distinguishing between acts which are good and those which are bad." [17]

Is one then entirely void of any notion with respect to what love demands? It is true that every new decision is called for in the light of its own unique circumstances and that, therefore, no inflexible rule or guide for right decision-making may be supposed as the sole (or even most important) criterion for determining or shaping duty. But one comes to every new moral decision with the resources of both principles and judgments that have been formulated in previous decisions. Neither value system nor situation can thus be said to be autonomous in the decisive moment; and what love *is,* experientially and conceptually, will then shape how one is to *do* it, and vice versa. The situationist is correct in saying that obligation in the situation cannot be identified with objectively "right" acts; nevertheless, I want to argue that one ought to *try* to decide what is right or good in this objective sense. The "deposit" of value judgments brought to new moments of decision cannot be either dismissed or given inferior status in the decision-making process.

Christian ethics traditionally has been thought to be inseparable from a religious milieu in which God has something to do with the meaning of right and wrong, good and bad, and from which the moral norms that assess human conduct derive. Whether the neighbor is helped or hurt may not depend upon reason operating apart from the religious tradition; that is, whether self or neighbor gets what he wants out of this decision/act. Moreover, love cannot be exercised in isolation as an insulated relationship between either the self and God or the self and neighbor. Agape always expresses itself in koinonia and *diakonia* as authentic *leitourgia*. How the neighbor is (to be) treated must therefore be formulated and assessed with reference to God's intention for him. That the neighbor is to be loved and what it means to love him are, it would then seem, antecedent to doing it. The error of the situationist approach probably lies in the extravagance rather than the exclusiveness of its claim that "Christian action should be tailored to fit objective circumstances, the *situation*." [18] In either case it promises more than it can produce. For if alternative courses of action are judged according to the circumstances of the existential moment and one's possibility for transcending this limitation be excluded, then freedom becomes only a solicitous platitude and one is victimized by the most brutal kind of contextual and impersonal determinism.

A final comment needs to be made about the functional worth of a value system (as I think the situationist's "non-system" to be) that is derived from precommitments to pragmatism, positivism, and relativism. Fletcher states,

"The situationist holds that whatever is the most loving thing in the situation is the right and good thing. It is not excusably evil, it is positively good." [19] Thus, if a lie be told unlovingly, it is wrong; but, if it be told in love, it is good.[20]

It has long been recognized that we often are confronted by a limited range of act-possibilities over which we exercise little or no control, but it has not been argued before that necessity in the form of situational problematics can make otherwise ambiguous choices Christianly and positively good. The empirical and casuistical temper of situationism has led it at this point to a value theory that is both unwarranted and untenable.

It is unwarranted because the range of moral understanding is not exhausted by assuming that what appears to be most loving under the circumstances can be called positively good. It cannot be consistently maintained, for example, that "killing 'innocent' people might be right." [21] Killing innocent people—if in modern wartime situations any portion of the population may any longer be described at really "innocent"—may be unavoidable; it may even seem to be relatively good, as the better course to take among limited alternatives; but it cannot be assigned unambiguous moral value. Rather, if justification by grace be taken seriously, one need not exonerate oneself from moral responsibility by calling equivocal acts right or positively good. Their contingent and provisional character can be recognized and accepted for what it is; namely, morally ambiguous, however necessary. Indeed, this fact can be appreciated as simply a constant reminder of man's creatureliness and his continual need for grace and pardon in the decision-making process. Forgiveness, morally understood, permits us to live without the choices we would have preferred but did not have. It is precisely this quality of the moral life that one misses in the situationist's baptism of existential necessity within the waters of normative relativism.

The value theory at issue here is also untenable because it establishes the base for the methodological model upon the exceptional case. Although the method of situation ethics is introduced with deference to the place of principles in the decision-making process, every case cited by Fletcher as illustrative of the situational approach demonstrates abandonment of generally accepted moral maxims. For example, he relates parallel stories of two women whose crying children threatened the safety of their respective wagon trains moving west in the eighteenth century. One mother (interestingly identified as a Negro) killed her baby with her own hands, and she and her companions reached the sanctuary of the fort; the other mother (a Scot) tried unsuccessfully to quiet her baby, and she and her party were discovered and destroyed by Indians. The altogether rhetorical question, "Which woman made the right decision?" is much too simplistic in its implied answer. Moreover, what is suggested here is elsewhere condemned; namely, generalizing value judgments without careful scrutiny of the whole range of contextual configurations. But, beyond all else, it is not inconceivable to me that a whole group of people might deliberately choose almost certain death (whether at the hands of Indians, Nazis, or the KKK) rather than submit to an existence bought at the price that would reduce human life to the law of the jungle.

Situationism emerges from legalism and extemporism as a corrective to the excesses of both; because of it, moralists who have been at ease in the Zion of either

103

pietism or existentialism will be less and less comfortable. We must still search for a way of doing ethics which overcomes the bifurcation between agape and eros, sacrificial and mutual love, and offers a viable prospect of God's love for his creation becoming enfleshed in that creation itself.

LOVE: CREATIVE RISK-TAKING

It may be appropriate that we continue to distinguish among the threefold expression of love as agape, eros, and philia; but it is a frequent and unfortunate fact that these distinctions are made in such a way as to perpetuate a radical discontinuity among them. When agape is defined as undifferentiated affection for an *other*, independent of the other's attractiveness or of some mutual interest, and when agape is thus juxtaposed to eros and philia, which in turn are supposed to depend upon these precise stimuli for the self's response, then the stage is set for a doctrine that is mistaken both theologically and psychologically. It is theologically faulty because it effectively denies any intelligible intercourse between God and the world; and it is psychologically fallacious because it makes normative a model for loving which is essentially schizophrenic. Agape does not substitute for eros or philia; indeed, the Christian understands it to be the implicit basis for both. Moreover, agape provides the context for the expression of these other kinds of love which fortifies, invigorates, and gives a measure of permanence to them. In sum, agape is obedience to the will of God in service to the neighbor. Approached in this way, eros and philia are not at all devalued. Instead, agape both depends upon these expressive means for its own embodiment and sustains them beyond those moments when otherwise they would falter or expire. Translated into the language of theology, this is simply acknowledgment that God's activity and purpose in incarnation is neither contradictory of nor discontinuous with his activity and purpose in creation.

There is no doubt that human sinfulness corrupts the essential spirit and intention of man's love and that the object of his love is similarly limited and ambiguous. But this "no" to the possibility of humanly expressing agape must not go unqualified; a sharp and irrevocable disjunction need not be made between God's work of redemption and the variety of activities in human culture. Somehow the awareness of God's reconciling presence must be recaptured in such a way as to affirm that his work of redemption does include a place of sharing and value for human creative effort, and that the kingdom of God is not absolutely separated from those imperfect goods for which men strive. *Sola gratia* permits the "no" to be balanced with a "yes," for it instructs us that acceptance does not depend upon the functional worth of strategy or the expediency of prudential wisdom. It is precisely at this point that the risk factor in human decision-making becomes viable. Reinhold Niebuhr and others have ably demonstrated the omnipresence of ambiguity and uncertainty in decision-making. Only naïveté or indifference could permit anyone in our time to ignore this fact and its corollary—that there is an irreducible element of risk in every moment when choices are made and acts committed.

I suggested at the beginning of this chapter that every ethical system (or nonsystem!) that fails to deal adequately with the reality of creative risk-taking is deficient both humanly and theologically. Now I am prepared to say that neither legalism, extemporism, nor situationism offers a competent and satisfactory human style of life. Each of these ways overlooks the reality of risk *within* the decision-making act, chiefly because each is absolute in its own way and thereby relieves man of genuine risk and responsibility. Built into these approaches is the assumption that risk means falling outside the system. In legalism, the risk is to fall away from grace if the law is not obeyed. In extemporism and situationism the risk is to fall into "the world" or into the "they-self" (*Das Mann*) or into "*mauvais fois.*"

Put differently, the place of risk in all three positions is extrinsic to the positions themselves, coming into the system as consequential to *not* doing the "good." The risk is the risk of falling; and therefore the risk is not within the act, having its meaning within the act, but lies in consequence of the act and has its meaning in terms of results. The act itself—the choice—is not one that includes risk as a constitutive part of the decision; that is, of the definition of the "good." Whatever else these positions offer by way of commending themselves, the fact that they pass over risk, which is within both the decision itself and the definition of the "good," makes them fundamentally non-human, if not indeed anti-human, ways of doing ethics.

What this comes down to, in the last analysis, is that both legalism and extemporism (together with situationism) are products of a nihilistic outlook. It is not insignificant that the devaluing of the world, which is a motif common to both, corresponds with an anti-creation motif. The "world" is objectified wickedness for the legalist and objectified meaninglessness for the extemporist. In both cases man is effectively nullified; and this, in turn, nullifies God (at least God as he is biblically understood).[22]

What love intends, Christianly speaking, is the same whether the loving subject is God or man. It may be described as the kingdom of God or the kingly rule of God's intention in the life of his creation. The biblical witness is that a person shows love or does what love intends in the measure to which his decisions, acts, and energies are devoted to expressing the sovereign reign of God in all human relationships. There are unquestionably certain dangers toward anthropomorphizing God in this way of speaking, but they are not in principle novel if God's enfleshment of himself in Jesus is taken seriously. Indeed, there is a sense, as Günther Bornkamm rightly suggests, in which "one cannot speak of love in too human, too 'anthropomorphic' a way. Only then is the full wonder apparent, that God's longing becomes his self-giving." [23]

Augustine usually can be cited to support either side of a controversial question; this one is no exception to the rule. He surely believed that concupiscence was the vehicle by which original sin was transmitted to the race and that every man, as Adam's progeny, was victimized by this heritage. But he also knew that the good which the kingdom of God intends is an inclusive good, seeking to transform self-interest in whatever form to God's good for the self. Hubris need not (nor can it, in light of God's reconciling activity in Christ) be taken as the last word (nor even the first word!) about man's affective consciousness. And even though self-assertion and pride do corrupt love's intention, agape is nevertheless a possibility in the measure to which an individual acknowledges God's intention for himself and the neighbor.

For what God in Christ reveals is nothing less than our authentic good, the meaning and purpose of creation. The clue to the nature of this good, as Daniel Day Williams puts it, is that "the love which is revealed in Christ is a love which seeks the fulfillment of all things in such a relationship to one another that what flows from the life of each enriches the life of all, and each participant in the whole life finds his own good realized through the giving of self to the life of the whole." [24] When I will the good of another, by that act of willing, his good becomes a good for me or, simply, my own good; and if that other be God, the willing of his good for me corresponds precisely with participation in his agape.

There is thus no radical bifurcation of meaningful relationship between divine and human modes of showing love. Acknowledgment of the cosmic consequences of God's presence in history, incarnate in Jesus, permits us to recognize that the locus of our existence is a profoundly transformed *mundus* in which the clue to our situation and destiny is not that we are the bastard offspring of a faithless Adam, but that we are sons and heirs with Christ. Where we are, historically and existentially, is in grace; if we find ourselves in sin, it is because we have opted for it despite God's decision for us. Our failure to love is in the truest sense, therefore, a denial of our real situation and not, as it has so long been supposed, an affirmation of it. What the world and man have long awaited in labor and travail is, in Christ, a present existential fact. God accepts the world, claims it, and reconciles it to himself.

Christ enters the world, taking up its history into himself and fulfilling it; and in that act a process of humanization is initiated which continues to animate our effort to embody that perfect humanity which he reveals. Fr. John Dourley has made the point succinctly:

> Such a theology of man's progressive humanization initiated by Christ on earth and prolonged in history under the impetus of his Spirit is fundamentally incompatible with an eschatology that would minimize the Christian's commitment to his society in the interests of his supernatural life. On the contrary it seems to unite the Christian's secular activity with his specifically religious life.[25]

Such an acknowledgment of God's decision for the world brings with it a genuine moral and religious revolution. Legal religion emphasizes what God demands and what man does; situational extemporism focuses on what man wants and how he gets it. Biblically, the emphasis is upon what God in Christ does, and the consequences of this mighty act for the conduct of human life—consequences that are formulated in terms of correspondence and continuity between God's intention for kingly rule in the heart of man and the expression of this intention in human conduct. Grace and judgment are inextricably bound up together. It is only a reminder of our creatureliness that judgment always accompanies decision-making, that concretizations of love are always imperfect, that risk always is part of the human situation. And it is similarly a reminder of the presence of a Creator in our history that the inevitability of risk in decision-making does not engender diffidence and paralysis.

How does one know that he is showing love in a situation? If Christ be acknowledged as model or paradigm, it would follow that this knowledge is commensurate with the measure to which one obediently expresses the will of God in service to the neighbor. The act that expresses this love may be inept, even infelicitous, as all of us know;

109

but it is only clumsy and not malevolently intentioned. It is a passionate and purposive involvement in the life of the beloved and knows nothing of indifference or nonchalance or disinterest. The lover gives himself to the beloved, and this is unmistakably risky business. But that is the very character of love—it makes one vulnerable to the neighbor, unprotected both from the neighbor's needs and those ways in which he chooses to reciprocate or retaliate. The paradigm, the model, is acknowledged by Christians to be God's gift of himself. "In this is love, not that we loved God but that he loved us and sent his Son to be the expiation for our sins" (1 John 4:10). That, too, one ventures to say, involved a risk. I would even suggest that not only is man saved by grace but that in some sense God also is "saved" to us by grace—he is surrounded in his own decision-making to create and become incarnate by his own grace. If creation and incarnation say anything about God, they certainly express his desire and intention for some reciprocal relationship between himself and his creation. But this again involves a certain risk. To put it rather crudely (with some risk!), if man has a problem without God, so does God have a problem without man.

In such a way as this, love incarnate becomes a distinct human possibility. Moreover, to take seriously the incarnation is to acknowledge that agape is the implicit premise for every instance of human affection. Agape knows no limit amid the manifold and chaotic conditions of existential life.

Of course, it is scandalous to talk this way—that is, of God's love particularizing and concretizing itself in human life—but this is so because even self-conscious obedience to God's will does not eventuate in moral action that escapes judgment or that can be said to be unequivocally

110

good. We may reasonably accept full responsibility for what we know in advance to be morally ambiguous choices and actions only in the measure to which we acknowledge God's presence in the flux and change of the moral struggle. This means that we know forgiveness while living within the frustrations of equivocal decision-making; that we can accept the apparent necessity of certain risks without having to justify the necessity.

This, while incomplete and provisional, nevertheless seems to me a more adequate way to approach both the theological issues and the human dimension of risk-action. At least the epistemological problems can begin to be resolved in terms of the scholastic notion of truth as *adequatio*, adequate to reality.

We are, as it were, pilgrims for whom progress toward the realization of God's purpose for our lives cannot be a solitary enterprise. We cannot forsake the "earthly city," as Augustine called it; nor can we hope to take with us all its citizens to the "celestial city." We work and serve in the persevering hope that the kingdoms of this world will, in fact, be translated into the kingdom of our God and of his Christ. Our unique peril is that we will ignore the moral claims that somehow seem to lie outside an arbitrarily limited area, and suppose our own wisdom and probity to have the intellectual and moral character appropriate for the inheritance of the kingdom of God.

6

Situational Morality

How is ethical function related to moral laws?

ROBERT W. GLEASON, S.J.

The new ethics—also called situational morality—is less a system than a widespread existential approach to Christian morality. Its authors are inspired partly by a revolt against what they consider the juridicism of traditional morality and partly by a desire to return to a more biblical pedagogy of morals. Frequently this new morality betrays itself more as an indefinable spirit than as a clear-cut theology or philosophy of morals. Condemning what it believes to be a common abuse of traditional morality —the attempt to make the juridical sphere the exemplary cause for all morality—the new ethics claims to be more fully Christian. It is only, we are told, through fully exploring the depth and the mystery of personal life that we

---

Robert W. Gleason, S.J., is professor of theology at Fordham University, New York.

can arrive at anything like a valid moral judgment. In taking into account this personal mystery, the new ethics would reject what it considers oversimplifications in the traditional morality.

BASIC CLAIMS OF SITUATION ETHICS

The distinctive claim of this new school of ethics is that it aims at placing man in the uniqueness of the given moment, before God his Father in an I-Thou relationship of love. Given that relationship, the decision that is proper in the unique set of circumstances should inevitably follow for the sincere Christian, guided as he is by an "inner light." But this decision will be formed ultimately not so much by the application of universal laws, such as the Ten Commandments, to a given situation, as by this mysterious inner light. The real concrete conditions in which one must make a moral decision are the circumstances which help the sincere Christian perceive what it is that God expects of him at the moment. Universal laws are of less importance in difficult cases, and may be bypassed with impunity, for the state of affairs in which man finds himself is unique and valid but once, and therefore general principles cannot fully command man's decisions. What the Christian needs above all things, the new ethicians believe, is sincerity, candor; less important are the objective actions that flow from this unconditioned sincerity.

It appears to some of the new theorists that the traditional morality has produced a bourgeois type of Christian with a legalistic mentality that is little conformed to the dictates of New Testament revelation. The accusation of "Old Testament" mentality has been leveled against those who insist upon the validity and necessity of juridical concepts in morality. Traditional morality has been accused of being a morality "of acts" that ignores the more fundamental orientations of the moral life and thus, through depersonalizing it, deprives the moral life of continuity and depth.

The new ethics insists strongly upon the need for a personal encounter between the deciding soul and its God at the moment of moral decision. Appeal to casuistry is depreciated as though casuistry has become the art of minimizing legal obligations. At times situational ethics finds traditional morality insufficiently demanding, at times insufficiently flexible. The root trouble seems to be, according to the new morality, the difficulty of exploring a concrete situation by universal laws. Without denying the existence of an objective moral order, this "morality of the spirit of the law" seeks to determine the objective morality of a given situation quasi-independently of abstract moral principles. It claims to be an existentialist, personalist morality in opposition to a merely "metaphysical" morality. Basically, since man is never found in the abstract, it contends that principles abstracted from his nature are never the ultimate determinant of the moral good for existent man. In a given situation man must find the objective moral order not by looking outside himself to abstract principles but by consulting his own spirit in confrontation with the God of revelation. Thus, it is hoped, man will be freed from certain insoluble conflicts which the present teaching of Christian morality imposes upon him. It would seem, too, that the proponents of these theories have not a very high opinion of the ordinary magisterium of the church in her ordinary decrees. Traditional morality has always insisted upon certain absolutes from which no exemption is possible. This is the point of separation from the new morality, which would insist that in a conflict between "personal values" and a course of action declared intrinsically wrong, the just man will spontaneously perceive that the intrinsically evil action is permitted to him. Traditional moral theology would not, of course, agree with such a course of action, but then, the proponents of the new theories feel that moral theology has allowed itself to be corrupted by unquestioning acceptance of principles drawn from such sources as pagan ethics and pre-Christian law. The result, it is supposed, is a morality that does not adequately represent the spirit of the gospel.

This latest attempt to renew the science of moral theology in the light of existentialist philosophy and the enhanced importance modern thought lends to subjective states and situational factors has merited the attention of the Holy See on more than one occasion. Finally it has drawn an instruction from the Holy Office forbidding its teaching by Roman Catholics. On February 2, 1956, the Holy Office issued an instruction condemning situational ethics as containing many things contrary to right reason, showing traces of modernism and relativism, and opposed to traditional Roman Catholic morality. Its teachings, under whatever name, are forbidden in Roman Catholic universities, seminaries, books, periodicals, conferences, or in any other fashion. Previous to this condemnation of the Holy Office, Pope Pius XII had spoken against situational ethics in his allocution to the World Federation of Catholic Young Women.[1]

115

THE ROLE OF THE INDIVIDUAL

It is undeniable that Christian activity today is rendered more difficult by a variety of social, economic, and cultural factors. While traditional morality has always taken these factors into consideration in its determination of the correct course of action that the Christian should assume, the new morality, or circumstance ethics, would give a far more compelling role to the individual and situational factors than has been admitted in the past.

One distinctive sign of the new morality is that conscience no longer has the function of transmitting law to the individual, but is regarded purely as a source of decision. The new morality prides itself on not being based exclusively upon commandments, particularly those of the Old Testament, nor upon laws, but upon the existential context in which a decision must be made. The individual must judge and choose within a network of circumstances that cannot be duplicated, and the absolute law, while not deprived of its value and adequacy in the objective order, is deemed insufficient enlightenment to the individual in difficult circumstances. Each act is to take place in a set of circumstances that is completely new and unrepeatable and, consequently, the call of God in this situation is one that is not fully covered by the objective, universal law based upon the abstract essence of man. Although the law in the abstract is valid, the existential context as determinant of genuine morality is superior to this law.

Whether a personal decision is taken as a conclusion of ethical reflection or as a sort of mystical inspiration purporting to come from the interior Master as guide for difficult situations, the result is that in practice the law is no longer considered as an ultimate source of ethical decisions.

The situational ethician has no intention of denying all objective validity to ecclesiastical legislation or to objective moral laws. His contention is rather that these laws may suffer exceptions in their obliging function. The question is rather whether the laws, for example, that govern marital conduct actually have obliging force in certain unusual and difficult situations. The principles that forbid extramarital relations are accepted by the situational ethicians as valid, but admitting of exceptions in those cases where they would foster genuine "interpersonal values." The commandment "Thou shalt not kill" would be accepted as obliging, except in extreme cases. A unique situation is conceived of as capable of legitimizing an exception to existing and valid laws. Such tendencies as these are rarely systematically exposed as a theory by the new ethicians. The new ethics rather poses the age-old question of the relationship of the individual to the universal and it rests upon a philosophy that does not wish to recognize structures universally applicable to each human being. Many of the authors who indulge in situational thinking do not espouse all the principles of situational ethics; they pick and choose, and in some authors it is rather an attitude of mind than a series of principles. Those who urge that not only general principles but also the concrete circumstances of both subject and object be taken into consideration in forming a moral judgment are, of course, not situational ethicians, since classical morality has always demanded this.

The leading European moralist of situation ethics is perhaps Eberhard Grisebach, whose ethical work espouses the principal theses of situational ethics in a more complete form than does the work of most others. Again, certain philosophers have contributed ideas to the movement without being identified with it; for example, Martin Buber and Franz Ebner. Helmut Thielicke and Emil Brunner, both Protestants, are strongly influenced by situational ethics. One of the foremost exponents of situation ethics in the United States is Joseph Fletcher.

NATURAL LAW AND CONSCIENCE

The concept of moral law on which situation ethics is built is clearly one that is foreign to Roman Catholic thought. There does exist a natural law, and man is bound in conscience to observe that law, whose primary principles, at least, are clearly perceptible. In creating man God has given him a natural light of the intelligence by which he may know what is to be done and what is to be avoided in the moral sphere. This natural law is itself a participation in the eternal law, which exists in God himself. Concerning the more general precepts of this natural law, no man with normally developed intelligence can be invincibly ignorant. Moreover, this law is intrinsically and extrinsically immutable; that is to say, it cannot be directly changed, although it can be indirectly changed in the sense that a certain matter may no longer fall under the law. There are actions that are intrinsically wrong from their very nature, prescinding from any circumstance attaching to them. In these substantially evil actions, such as hatred of God, perjury, lying, no change whatsoever is possible in the law governing them. They are always and in every circumstance wrong. Certain actions require the presence of an added circumstance

118

for them to be called evil, and if the circumstance is not present, the action is not wrong.

The new morality, while it does not deny the existence of such a natural law, seems to feel that it is of secondary importance. In fact, some seem to think that if such a natural law exists and does not suffer exceptions, it partakes of the absolute character of God to such an extent as to become a second absolute alongside of God. Classical moral theology has always insisted that the ultimate criterion of moral goodness is the objective right order determined by the natural law and known with certitude from that law as applied to a particular set of circumstances according to the principles of prudence. Situational ethics prefers to think that man is not orientated in his ultimate decisions by objective and ontological law but by psychological, personal, innate lights.

At times the decision of the "awakened" conscience will be in full conformity with objective laws; at times it will not. Above all, we are told, one should avoid treating these laws as though they were a set of majors from which one could easily deduce the moral conclusion. Since each situation in which man finds himself is unique and irreducible to any combination of universal laws, it will require more than deduction to enlighten man as to his duty in a difficult set of circumstances. The individual should rather try to evaluate his particular situation in the light of the I-Thou relationship to the God of the New Testament and, in the light of this personal relationship, should come to a decision that will be valid only for this unique existent at this historical moment. Hence, although one would ordinarily judge an individual guilty of apostasy if he abandons his faith to join a false religion,

119

according to the existentialists one should rather qualify this as a good act if it responds to what the interior illumination of "conscience" suggests to the individual at the moment. Again, according to this school of ethicians, one must leave the Christian conscience free, in marital matters, to decide what will sponsor and promote the personal values of marriage, even if this be at the expense of the offspring.

Such statements as these, at first hearing, seem strange enough to the Christian accustomed to evaluate moral acts upon the basis of universally binding principles. These statements manifest a curious confusion as to the function of the individual conscience. Obviously man is obliged to follow his conscience, even when it is erroneous. But, on the other hand, he is also obliged to attempt to form his conscience correctly. Conscience certainly dictates what the individual is to do in each particular situation, but it also expresses the moral demands of human nature as such. It is obviously the task of educators to see that the Christian conscience is adult, but adulthood does not mean liberation from universal norms based upon the unchanging nature of man himself and, finally, the nature of God himself. The situational ethician seems to feel, at least in extreme cases, that the Christian conscience cannot be bound by the law of nature or the law of the decalogue, which God has entrusted to human authority to conserve and explain. On the contrary, Christian ethics has always insisted that the moral order is constructed upon the order of being, of existence. The ultimate norm for human conduct in the natural order is the being of man and ultimately the being of God, the absolute norm of perfection. Man's being, that is, his nature according to its constitutive elements and its essential relations to God, man, and the universe, is the proximate norm for determining his moral activity. It is not the personal persuasion of the subject acting which is the decisive norm of ethical action. No one denies that the role of situation and circumstances is of considerable importance in moral decisions. But, again, this role is not to be determined by some mystical intuition of the subject. The particular circumstances of the action have their determined existence which can be known by the intelligence, and norms drawn from them can be used in forming a moral judgment.

AN ETHICS OF CONFRONTATION

The new theory, while admitting the existence of universal laws, and even using them in the formation of a practical judgment, refuses to grant them the ultimately decisive role that they have played in traditional Christian ethics. Thus, although one may admit that in ordinary circumstances suicide, onanism, direct abortion would be wrong, *for the reasons offered by traditional morality,* the new ethics would deny that this general rule should be the ultimate and decisive factor in a moral decision. The man who is placed in a particular concrete situation will be able to perceive (and they do not mean by this an invincibly erroneous conscience) that in this particular situation onanism, direct abortion, suicide, is objectively licit, despite the fact that the general objective moral order forbids it. The defenders of this theory, in other words, allow a dependent, conditioned validity to the objective moral order. The objective moral laws have

121

their proper validity, but the ultimate moral decision of man cannot be made solely on the basis of their application to a particular case.

Instead, this new theory demands an eminently individual and personal ethics: an ethics of confrontation. The individual must confront his personal God and in a dialogical situation with God he is to make his choice. In many cases this individual choice will not be measured by any objective norm. In many cases the objective norm will suffice; the presumption ahead of time is that it *will* suffice. In those cases that directly flow from the unchanging metaphysical nature of man, the objective norm may ultimately have the decisive word. Thus it would not be true to say that this new theory of ethics has as its purpose to overthrow the general principles of objective ethics, or the decalogue. Rather it wishes to question the *absolute* value of the principles and submit them to a more decisive principle. This more decisive principle is the meeting of man with God the Father and the illumination of the human conscience that the situational ethicians assume will follow.

The authors of this system rely heavily upon those spiritual intimations that directors of conscience are accustomed to refer to as "movements of spirits" or intimations of the Holy Spirit. These evidently do not depend upon a syllogistic process for a determination of their validity. But neither do their conclusions run counter to the dictates of objective morality. The examples that the situational ethicians adduce of extreme cases are nothing new in moral theology. But the principle of immediate illumination is one that ultimately resolves itself into the principle of strong subjective conviction about that which is licit and illicit. Secular experience proves that strong subjective convictions can also lead to strange conclusions. Either the defenders of situational ethics are to judge their illuminations by objective norms or they are to leave them without further justification. The rules for discernment of spirits to which these authors appeal, while not applied with syllogistic rigor, are nonetheless firmly based upon the objective order of things as known by experience. It is precisely the internal persuasion which needs objective guarantees of its validity and not vice versa. The notion of an internal intuition of the moral good at times betrays a rather confused epistemology. Certainly, in the experience of objective reality, primitive and intuitive judgments play a role. No ethician wishes to reduce all interpretation of reality to forms of deduction and induction. But those judgments concerning internal facts which are called intuitive are objectively valid not because of the strength of the personal persuasion of the subject but because they are immediately known as expressions of the objective order quite independent of the subject's persuasion. There are also judgments of reality that are direct rather than reflex and that correspond to the subject's habitual knowledge of a certain question, although the reasons for this judgment cannot be immediately proffered. But again these judgments are not in conformity with being *because* the subject is so persuaded but because the subject has a primitive or intuitive judgment of their conformity to objective reality. They may not be demonstrated syllogistically, but can be confirmed by metaphysical reflection or indirectly. The criterion of their truth is their conformity with reality and not with an internal persuasion.

The ultimate decisive norm of this ethics is not the application of an objective law to a particular case but the immediate internal light which may or may not be in conformity with objective law. No external rule measures the validity of this internal judgment, neither experience, nor principle, nor nature. The internal light is fully self-sufficient. Previous to the moral decision the mind may indeed reflect upon the general and specific moral principles of objective ethics, but these do not enter into the decision itself; rather that is dictated by an innate habitual disposition fitted to the individual personality and permitting him to perceive what line of moral conduct is exactly adapted to his entire personality. The ethical value in question is not deduced by some comparison with an extrinsic norm but grasped by introspection upon the individual personality. What is important to underscore is that the result of this introspection is said not merely to be subjectively licit but *objectively* good. Neither is the situation such that the individual may generalize the results of this introspection into some kind of a general norm for procedure in the future. Each individual moment is unique and requires and finds its own insight.

In its exaggerated form this existential ethics condemns all restrictions from outside authority such as the law of the decalogue, the community of the church. What counts is not so much the conformity or nonconformity to objective law or ecclesiastical decisions as the profound sincerity of the subject. God is interested primarily in the intention, and this counts before the objective value of the action. Such an exaggerated separation of the order of intention and execution in the name of authentic sincerity is, of course, indefensible.

The new theory would claim for itself certain advantages in the formation of the Christian conscience. It

124

claims that the filial relationship to God which is revealed in the New Testament is fostered psychologically by this person-to-person confrontation with God our Father. The endless ratiocinations that ordinary moral theology would impose upon the sincere subject are presumed to be dispensed with by appeal to the basic light revealing the call of God in each individual situation. Both extremes, laxity and scrupulosity, should normally be obviated by recourse to the presence of the God before whom the subject takes his decision.

The ultimate differences between this new morality and traditional morality come down to this: In an objective system of ethics the moral judgment is submitted to an extrinsic norm, an ontological norm founded on the principles of being. In situational ethics the moral judgment is measured only by the subjective, immanent light of the individual in question.

Since the ultimate decisive factor in situational ethics is the internal "judgment" of the subject, it is easy to see that situational ethics can be exaggerated in either direction: laxity or severity. The internal personal light may be interpreted either as an exemption from the objective moral law or as an imposition of an added obligation. The argument claims that man will be enabled spontaneously and immediately to recognize the voice of God dispensing or obliging. The classic rules for discerning extraordinary calls from God are not so optimistic. They require careful comparison of the "call" with objective norms governing conduct and objective norms concerning human psychology. Subjective conviction is never accepted as any guarantee for the objective existence of a privileged experience, vocation, or exemption. Depth psychology, clinical psychology, and psychoanalysis have established certain objective norms by which subjective experience may be measured and examined, and classical moral theology appeals to such objective norms in extraordinary cases, and not to the immediate intuition of the subject, as a guarantee of objectivity. On the principles of situational ethics, it is quite impossible to make a scientific judgment on the validity of the invitations of God that it supposes. There is no argument either from the traditional norms of spiritual direction or from the discoveries of scientific psychology that can be drawn in favor of the value of the situational intuitions.

There can be no doubt that situational ethics, at least in its extreme forms, is freighted with relativism. While it does not deny the existence of immutable ethical principles founded upon the nature of man, it does resolve the moral judgment, not into fixed principles of objective validity but into the self-sufficient internal light of the subject. The personal intuition that is characteristic of this system is not the *unique* norm for action but it is the decisive norm. In its appeal to a certain affinity with the moral good in question, impervious to the examination of reason, situational ethics resembles somewhat the "moral sense" of the modernists. It manifests an exaggerated confidence in what man "feels" or "judges," and an exaggerated understanding of the principle of immediate communication between God and man. Thus the written law of God, communicated to man through divinely appointed authority, is relegated to a position of secondary importance. The guidance of the church is, if not rejected, minimized.

The insistence upon sincerity of intention and the formation of an adult conscience is certainly justified, but sincerity of intention does not suffice to make an action

126

objectively good. The action that follows upon a good intention should also be conformed to all the divine and natural laws that are involved in the particular situation. Nor is it ever permitted to do evil in order that good may result. It is evident that there are situations in Christian life which require heroism of the Christian. The martyrs of the past and the present show full awareness of this fact, refusing appeal to situational techniques to avoid responsibility.

It is quite obvious that in moral action the circumstances are also to be considered, and a lengthy science has been elaborated by moralists for taking care of just this need. The Thomistic doctrine of prudence contains the essential good offered by the doctrine of situational ethics. Traditional morality has always recognized the need for exemptions, excusing causes, epikeia in particular situations with regard to positive laws. But absolutes also exist and there is no dispensation permitting actions intrinsically wrong, such as blasphemy, direct abortion, onanism. In its most extreme form circumstance ethics contains many philosophical errors. In its distaste for obligations connected with juridical bonds, it attempts to dissolve the obligation character that accompanies every moral value because of the connection of such values with the supreme goodness of God. The fact that obedience to the law involves struggle and difficulty does not deprive obedience of its moral character. The fullness of affective response to the situation at hand is something that is not always at the direct disposition of the subject and to claim that morality is valueless without this response is to ignore the character of this response and reduce it to the level of mere feelings.

It is, moreover, impossible to eliminate from ethics all

general principles. The individuating notes that go to make up individual human nature do not change its essential oneness. It is precisely the existence of general laws of morality which makes it possible to cope with an individual situation. Lacking them the individual is left without any governing norms for his unique case. The fact that each situation is unique does not invalidate the general law but invites to an application of that law. Hence the importance of the much-despised casuistry attacked by the situational ethicians. If abstract principles of morality can be casually put aside in difficult cases, the complexity of the personal situation is not being adequately evaluated; it is simply being denied. General moral principles are always supposed in any call that God addresses to the individual soul. Confrontation with the God of revelation does not dissolve the commandments written by his creative act in our human nature which we possess in common with the rest of men. While the religious man has indeed the task of finding out what the will of God invites him to do in his unique situation, he begins by presupposing that God's will is not in contradiction with itself as revealed in nature and in the decisions of his church, the prolongation of the incarnation.

Situational ethics is really a more refined form of relativism, for while admitting the validity of general principles, it does not admit that they are ultimate or absolute. What we would need then is a continual source of revelation for the guidance of our moral life. The result would be a far greater legalism than that from which situational ethics claims to relieve us. We would be left with no general principles of guidance and reduced to a blind acceptance of the private illumination repeatedly given but without intelligible relation to any outside norms.

Christian morality is the fulfillment of natural morality, but it is not its destruction. The fact that a principle is historically derived from Roman law or Aristotelian philosophy does not prove that it is an unchristian principle. Nor is the natural law abrogated by a filial relationship to God, who is also the author of nature.

While the motive of love is a noble one, it is not in Christian tradition to present it as the exclusive motive for moral action. Nor will Christianity ever accept a system of morality which attacks the fundamental notion of a revealed morality possessing the authoritative guidance given to defend that revelation.

The subjectivism and relativism that are in some degree implicit in situational ethics make it quite unacceptable to the Christian mind, even though the excellent intentions and partial intuitions of the system may be admired.

7

The Nature of Heresy

Can part of the truth be substituted for all of it?

GERALD KENNEDY

The mention of heresy will sound to most moderns as outgrown and probably ridiculous. It has become something of a badge of honor to be regarded as a heretic, and most younger men who are discussing Christian theology and Christian ethics will pay as much attention to this label as they would to an accusation of being progressive. But that there are rules, principles, and guidelines which lead to salvation while aberrations result in damnation will get very little serious attention today. The heretic usually carries with him a certain flamboyance which has great appeal to the rebel. Yet I dare to refer to heresy as false belief which so distorts a man's view of reality that it makes him unhappy and miserable. Our fathers, who were less squeamish, called it damnation.

Gerald Kennedy is bishop of The Los Angeles Area, The Methodist Church.

The Nature of Heresy

Heretics often have been very attractive persons. John Wesley found some of them to be kindred spirits, as will most Christians. They were not men who denied truth but only tried to substitute part of the truth for all of it. Their mistake was not falsehood so much as acceptance of what was partially true as being completely true. Often they were men of logical bent who found it impossible to hold seeming contradictions together.

The man who gave me my first insight into the nature of orthodoxy and the weakness of heresy was G. K. Chesterton, who in 1908 wrote a book called *Orthodoxy*.[1] Shortly after the appearance of Joseph Fletcher's *Situation Ethics*, I reread Chesterton's book. The thing that astounded me most was its freshness and relevance to the modern scene. His startling paradoxes may be carried too far at times and it seems now and then that Chesterton is drunk with them. But no man saw more dramatically the Christian clues to truth, symbolized not in a sphere, but in the rough, sharp angles of the cross. For him, morality was a dark and daring conspiracy. He came to Christian faith by way of a haunting conviction that its seeming contradictions were pointing to a larger synthesis. Not preachers or Christian apologists led him to Christ, but the atheist converted him to Christianity. It was the unbeliever and his arguments that sowed in his mind the first wild doubts of doubt.

One of the things that Chesterton is very careful to point out is the danger of taking a proposition, logical in itself, and then behaving as if it were the whole truth. Heresy is primarily a lack of balance, and this was the reason why the church through the years has fought for

131

what seemed to be a minor point here in order to preserve the larger truth there. It was no trouble for the Christian to believe that there was such a thing as fate but also that there was such a thing as free will. Nor was there any difficulty in his thinking in terms of the law while preaching the gospel of grace.

It is the logician who gets into trouble because life is almost logical but not quite. And so, if men are to find their way over the road of sanity to the goal of truth, they must not be afraid to hold two seeming opposites in mind at the same time. Above all, they must not believe that any truth can be pursued to its logical conclusion without being checked by its opposite. Virtues really go mad when they are isolated one from the other and are allowed to wander off alone. Chesterton pointed out that some scientists care for truth and their truth is pitiless, while some humanitarians care for pity, but it is the kind of pity that is often untruthful. The two have to be held together in tension.

I remember an old professor of mine who talked about "contrapletes." He said that there are matters which are only fully realized and completed by the truth of their opposites. I never knew whether this philosophy went very far, but it made a big impression upon me, and I have found it to be helpful and realistic. Through the years men have been emphasizing one aspect of reality and, so far as they go, it is fine. But sooner or later another aspect is demanded and the new age directs its attention to something that has been either forgotten or neglected. There is no better example of this than theology, which used to be referred to as the queen of the sciences.

Theologians make their way as a sailing ship which

132

always has to tack back and forth with and against the wind. It does not follow the straight line like a steamer, and any particular generation is either to the right or to the left of center. Its genius lies in having within itself the check against its own excesses. So, after theologians have gone so far, they know they have passed the main point and must come back. Then in their enthusiasm they will probably go too far in the other direction and sooner or later will have to come back again. This is the history of human thought, and the man who can take a look that is long enough will never be overly impressed with the popular teaching of his day. He will remember other times and other places where the same excess was popular before, and he will know that just as it had to come back in the past, it will have to come back again in the future. Incidentally, such a man takes with what patience he can muster the continuous and always false claim that somebody has a new theology, a new ethic, or a new morality.

The world is a place of limits, and ethics can never be made a simple matter of saying Yes. For every time a man says Yes to one thing, he has to say No to something else. These limits are really laws, if I may put it that way, and the man who does not like law is the man who does not like facts. But whether he likes them or not is of minor importance, for he has to deal with them and live according to their rules. Nor do I think that love has very much to do with this, but I shall say more about that later.

The man who wants to revolt must never suppose that he can revolt against everything. On that path he will come to futility. To be against things means one has to be for something. To say that we may deny all principles or laws and take our refuge in the impulses of the heart will take us into the land of anarchy where no road leads anywhere because all the landmarks are removed. Some sort of fixed and familiar boundary is necessary if there is to be a real revolution; otherwise we are in the position of the man who has made up his mind to be against everything and ends up being for nothing.

It is also true, I think, that so far as society is concerned, men will be in favor of fixed rules and clear dogmas if they want to protect the poor. Chesterton says that the rules of a club occasionally favor a poor member, but the drift of a club is always in favor of the rich one. Law is often the poor man's only protection. Anarchy is finally dull, while the man whose life is a great adventure usually travels in the land of authority.

Let me give what seems to me to be a wonderful Chesterton observation, and then I shall leave him, for a time at least:

> To have fallen into any one of the fads from gnosticism to Christian Science would indeed have been obvious and tame. But to have avoided them all has been one whirling adventure; and in my vision the heavenly chariot flies thundering through the ages, the dull heresies sprawling and prostrate, the wild truth reeling but erect.[2]

This sums up the man's position about as well as it can be in a few words. I am of the opinion that this is a point of view which will be very helpful in a day when we talk about situational ethics and the new morality. Maude Royden wrote an article many years ago on "Pagan Virtues and Christian Graces" in which she stated that when the Sermon on the Mount recommends humility, it always presupposes self-respect and that "every Christian grace was founded upon the rock of honor and loyalty,

134

courage and justice, a piercing vision, a great strength. It is only the strong who can really be gentle." What she was suggesting is something that is very easy to forget. When we Christians talk about a particular phase of Christianity, we are likely to forget that we must assume other characteristics which will hold it up. Christianity has always championed tenderness but never weak tenderness. It believes in forgiveness, but only when it is terrible as an army with banners. If we reduce all guidance to a single proposition, we fall into the trap of failing to recognize the reality of other elements which, if ignored, make our proposition partial and misleading.

FLETCHER ON ETHICS

Now let us take a look at Fletcher's book and report the effect that the reading of *Situation Ethics* had on a man who is neither a philosopher nor a theologian. I do not say this apologetically, because if there is any new light on ethics it ought to be discernible for the man who must deal with people within the framework of an institution. It is an easy book to read. Professor Fletcher writes with grace and light, which is rather unusual in a scholar. He dares make a point through an anecdote—and he tells at the beginning of a cab driver who was a longtime Republican but before an election had decided: "There are times when a man has to push his principles aside and do the right thing." That St. Louis cabbie, says the author, is the book's hero.[3] It did not seem to me, however, that what Professor Fletcher is saying is directed primarily toward this fellow.

Situation Ethics has both an element of calculation and an absolute element. The method is the calculating

135

part. In Edmond Cahn's phrase, "Every case is like every other case, and no two cases are alike." It is this unlikeness in similar cases which makes a rule or a law inadequate. The "situation" demands that a different principle be brought into play which is of course the principle of agape. The process to be followed in such a system is described as:

> (1) Its one and only law, agape (love), . . . (2) the Sophia (wisdom) of the church and culture, containing many "general rules" of more or less reliability, . . . (3) the kairos (moment of decision, the fullness of time) in which *the responsible self in the situation* decides whether the Sophia can serve love there, or not. This is the situational strategy in capsule form.[4]

Thus does Fletcher strive to escape the rule of law and also escape the condemnation of being antinomian, which would be a good trick if he could do it.

This means that every man has to decide ultimately according to his own estimate of conditions and consequences what should be done in a particular situation. There is the situation; there is the man; there is the decision. The authority of the decision does not rest on previous experience or in the wisdom of the race. This is where Fletcher would certainly differ with men who value tradition. Chesterton has what seems to me to be a great word here:

> Tradition may be defined as an extension of the franchise. Tradition means giving votes to the most obscure of all classes, our ancestors. It is the democracy of the dead. Tradition refuses to submit to the small and arrogant oligarchy of those who merely happen to be walking about. All democrats object to men's being disqualified by the accident of birth; tradition objects to their being disqualified by the accident of death. Democracy tells us not to neglect a good man's opinion, even if he is our groom; tradition

asks us not to neglect a good man's opinion, even if he is our father. I, at any rate, cannot separate the two ideas of democracy and tradition; it seems evident to me that they are the same idea. We will have the dead at our councils.[5]

What Fletcher seems to be about is to establish a relativism that is anchored to an unchanging principle or attitude or point of view. I think I am most troubled in failing to find any light on this unchanging principle which is called agape but tends to become more abstract than any moral law. Nor can I reach any other conclusion than that at the end of the day a man makes his decisions in the light of his own personal interpretation of what this agape demands. We hope he may prove adequate, but there is nothing in human experience to give a foundation for the hope.

The weakness of the book comes out most markedly when Fletcher is dealing with objections to his theory. He quotes Cicero: "Only a madman could maintain that the distinction between the honorable and the dishonorable, between virtue and vice, is a matter of opinion, not of nature." [6] Then he goes on to say that this is precisely and exactly what situation ethics maintains. But it is hard to see that it does maintain it and, on the contrary, it seems to deny it. He says also that one of the criticisms is that situationism ignores the reality of human sin and egocentricity and, indeed, that is exactly what I would say about it. I do not find any adequate answer to this objection. In answer to Nathaniel Micklem's story about an Indian giving away his fortune to the poor and leaving his creditors unpaid, Fletcher's answer is that justice and charity are the same thing and that the man made a mistake in his choice.[7] All this does is to indicate the funda-

137

mental weakness in the whole proposition that every man has to make up his mind in a particular situation without the guidance of a moral law.

One of the main themes of this book is the identification of love with justice. There runs through the whole writing an insistence that these are not two separate concepts but one. I can see that in an ultimate sense there may be truth in this, but I see also the impossibility of organizing a society without just laws which may now and then be unfair to an individual. Jesus warned against making judgments, and any man who is at all sensitive to the human plight knows that because of ignorance and sin ultimate judgment must be left to God. But it is also true that to institute individual choice for law is to accept a rule of men over a rule of principle. If it is necessary to make that choice, then I think it is better to accept law knowing that oftentimes it is unfair in a particular case rather than to eliminate the idea altogether. Concepts of the law should be kept wide and fluid enough to adjust to individual cases. It does not help me very much to have the author draw certain illustrations in particular instances where laws are unjust. In society it does not seem possible that we can escape this, the human situation being what it is. But my guess is that there will be less injustice by operating society within the framework of laws made as just as can be than by following the path Professor Fletcher suggests.

There is a reference to T. E. Lawrence who was leading Arab forces against the Turks.[8] Hamed the Moor killed Salem in a personal quarrel, which Lawrence had tried to stop. Now Lawrence knew that Salem's people would exact justice by revenge and that this would start an endless feud. What should he do? He killed Hamed to

138

end the affair. The implication is that this was justified and right because it prevented further bloodshed. It is almost exactly the same argument that was used by Americans when they dropped an atom bomb on Japan. When it is lifted up to that wider social context, the issue does not seem to be nearly so clear. Nor does it seem to me that we are in a position now to eliminate the old commandment "Thou shalt not kill" because a higher way has been found.

In another passage Fletcher tells of the late Alexander Miller's interviews with some of the French maquis after World War II. The maquis told of thievery and killings and, when asked if everything was permissible, their reply was, "Yes, everything is permitted—and everything is forbidden." [9] Very good. And yet to suggest this as a principle that will guide men in their actions seems like leaning on shadows. When men have gone to war—surely the most immoral activity that man endorses legally—they have already broken the moral law, and from that time on and within that context it is hard to find the ethical way under any circumstances.

I agree with Fletcher's criticism of Thomas Huxley's remark, made a century ago, that he would not mind being wound up like a clock if he could be assured that all his decisions would be correct and he could be freed of the burden of freedom. We must choose, and perhaps I speak only as one individual when I say that in that freedom to choose I do not want to be left entirely on my own, even with agape. I need something of the wisdom of the past and the experience of society which has been summed up in general principles.

Fletcher writes: "Is adultery wrong? To ask this is to ask a mare's-nest question. It is a glittering generality, like Oscar Wilde's mackerel in the moonlight: it glitters but it stinks. One can only respond, 'I don't know. Maybe. Give me a case. Describe a real situation.' " [10] Now this sounds very good to a man who may be in a classroom and is thinking only of a theoretical situation. It sounds quite different to the administrator of a church who has to deal with a thousand preachers and their families. Let me speak of situations out of my own experience.

I have not the slightest doubt that there are times when a case of adultery has all kinds of extenuating circumstances which may engage the sympathy of any man who knows the whole situation. One cannot sit in judgment upon a man or a woman who has gone over that line and simply say that all cases are the same. Quite so! But neither does a Methodist annual conference feel at ease in leaving the decision to an individual or a group of individuals with no general principle announced. If a man is all sympathy and the breaking of marriage vows is excused, every Methodist minister with a shaky marriage will try to come into his conference and sit under his mercy. If a man has no sympathy and is entirely legalistic in his interpretation, the minister or his wife having difficulty in this field will try to go somewhere else and find a more lenient atmosphere. So where I do my work, the annual conference has said that any man whose marital situation has deteriorated and reached public notice must take a different relationship with the conference. This is a rule. He may apply for restoration later on. There have been times when he has been restored. But to think that any man in a position of authority is wise enough or good enough or loves enough to decide these things without reference to law, seems nonsense. We are on much safer

and fairer grounds when we subscribe to the commandment "Thou shalt not commit adultery" and assume that
marriage is for always.

When one turns to the problem of sex relations in
youth, one finds the same problem and the same situation. What young man or young woman under the emotional pressure of a moonlight night or a particular
situation can be expected to have the judgment to take
the long look in such matters? Who in his early years can
begin to comprehend the terrifying, wonderful relationship between the sexes, which can produce joy and greatness and also despair and misery? These are situations
that demand guidelines and parental training according
to those lines. This is the place where, as Chesterton put
it, one needs the voice of the dead and the long, long
experience of the race. To eliminate all that and put in
its place what Fletcher terms agape is the heresy of taking part of the truth as the whole truth and thus con-
deming men to the loss of liberty.

That there are cases where abortion should be allowed
legally, I have no doubt. Society is wrestling with this
problem, constantly trying to find a way to allow this
freedom in exceptional cases without having it run loose
and become disastrous. That a mercy killing is at times
the only sensible thing is perfectly obvious to me. I am
not ready to say, however, that we should eliminate the
law which forbids it and trust to the good judgment of
doctors. I do not think any doctor in his right mind wants
to take that responsibility either. A way has to be found
along the narrow ridge between love on the one hand and
law on the other. Nothing in Fletcher's book seems to me
to have contradicted this truth.

Situation ethics is best summed up under the six propositions that Professor Fletcher announces as the foundations of his case.

1. "Only one 'thing' is intrinsically good; namely, love: nothing else at all." [11] This is all right except I think it depends a great deal on definition, and individuals do not always come to the same definitions of their terms. Also, I am bothered by that last phrase, "nothing else at all." This seems to be substituting one absolute for another. Dean Robert Fitch of the Pacific School of Religion, in an article in *Religion in Life,* writes:

> Personally I am leery of all love-absolutists. . . . If, moving in such company I should meet a Joseph Fletcher, then the encounter could be a pleasant and profitable one. But then, in such company, it is equally possible that I might run into the Grand Inquisitor.[12]

And as we go on through these six propositions, we can see how often Fletcher makes an absolute of what he says.

2. "The ruling norm of Christian decision is love: nothing else." [13] We Christians cannot doubt that the ruling norm in our decisions should be love, but Jesus never hesitated to add some directions and even put down some regulations that explain what this means in particular situations. These became rules.

3. "Love and justice are the same, for justice is love distributed, nothing else." [14] I wish I could believe that. I do not believe that history says this is true or that a look back into the way men have behaved in their societies would say it is true. Liberty seems to require a civil society and a bill of rights. To wipe this all out and say that to have faith and love as the beginning and ending of all human behavior and motivation is enough, is not realistic.

4. "Love wills the neighbor's good whether we like him

142

or not." [15] There is no debate here, I think, for this is good New Testament teaching. It is the Christian definition of what love is.

5. "Only the end justifies the means; nothing else." [16] If this means that love produces results by which one judges it, I agree. If this means that bad means cannot destroy good ends, I do not agree. If it implies that when a man's goal is right, he is free to do as he pleases to attain it, that is not true. If it does not mean any of these things, the proposition seems to be essentially meaningless in its present form.

6. "Love's decisions are made situationally, not prescriptively." [17] I like the idea of not deciding things in advance and I suppose this is what Professor Fletcher is saying. We must not be rigid and legalistic in all these matters. That, of course, was what many of the New Testament writers were saying when they attacked the Pharisees. But, at the same time, I cannot escape the feeling that there are written into the very nature of things certain principles that need to be learned before the actual crisis is met. To come up to a situation without any preparation in the way of general laws which one has assented to will not result in more justice; it will turn into more anarchy, and this is the part of the book that troubles me most. Granted, a man can go wrong by taking tradition too seriously. Granted, society ought not to be too rigid and unbending in its attitude toward the lawbreaker and the sinner. The answer is not to be found in eliminating all law and all tradition but in interpreting these things within the context of Christian love.

A CRITICISM

If *Situation Ethics* were an essay on love as the ultimate good or a discussion of the weakness of laws regarded as a final guide of behavior, I would read it with joy and accept it as a valuable testimony to the reality of the spirit of the Christian faith. But it is supposed to be a system of ethics and I assume it is meant to be the indication of a way by which men can live together and find freedom. This is where I leave it. Here is a book full of fine insights which are dissipated because the author absolutizes agape and eliminates the place of law. It may be a very practical way in heaven, but even with the most optimistic viewpoint I can muster, it seems little more than a one-sided view and a denial of a great body of experience whose loss this world could not possibly endure.

I have been impressed and a little frightened by the growing possibility of manipulating men's minds by drugs and "hidden persuaders." A people who fell under the control of ruthless and conscienceless tyrants would be at the mercy of powers that could direct them not only physically but also psychologically. May this never happen to us or to any nation. The threat, however, makes a framework of laws not less important but more necessary.

Ignoring this, I cannot escape the suspicion that Fletcher is assuming a situation which does not exist: that men who love have judgment enough to decide individual matters without harming their brethren. Even if the world were full of saints, which is obviously not the case, I would not want to be at the mercy of the decisions of some of the saints I have known. I do not doubt their good intentions and their pure motives, but I do doubt their judgment. God has not indicated thus far that when he

144

creates people who sincerely follow the law of love their choices will always be sensible so far as society is concerned.

Young people in a mood of rebellion, in any case, may find Fletcher's book justification for paying no heed to the words of their elders. They may find the reason they seek for ignoring all past wisdom and all prudent advice. I should not want to bear such a responsibility on the basis of anything that I have found in the book.

Too much is left to choice and to individual decision. I am sure that God judges men on the basis of the motives of their hearts. But man has learned out of experience that it is better to trust laws than to trust persons—good or bad. I do think that Christians must strive to attain the status of loving God perfectly as John Wesley argued in his doctrine of Christian perfection. But even such an attainment would not free society from the necessity of laws. This is the heresy of the Fletcher book.

Justice by its very nature has to deal with generalities. It has to deal with groups and societies. If love is just an individual matter between one man and another, outside the social context, that is fine. But it never is and cannot be. Therefore the general law is necessary to make society work at all. Situational ethics is certainly not new and the New Testament has plenty of testimony supporting what Fletcher is saying. But the New Testament never counsels cutting loose from the moral law the way this new book does. That is the reason why the New Testament speaks to man's condition today just as it did in the first century and why *Situation Ethics* will speak to a few situations in particular places without having universal significance.

Even when a man's heart is in the right place, I am not willing to trust his judgment regarding social relation-

145

ships. For these judgments which are so important are not dependent entirely upon the right point of view but upon experience and, for want of a better word, what I have always called "judgment." Good men do stupid things and the world may be on the right track when it refuses to turn over its affairs to the saints. Here is an example.

One of my young preachers had specialized in counseling until he was an expert in dealing with personal problems people brought to him. I know he was because he told me so. The only difficulty was that he had gone so far in one direction he had become somewhat like Professor Fletcher in eliminating all run-of-the-mill experience; for the good of a particular person, he ignored social laws. A married woman in his congregation had come to him for help, and he had been working with this "client" for some weeks. One day somebody opened the door of his study and found that he was kissing the lady. You can imagine the stir this caused not only on the part of the observer but upon those the observer shared his observations with. I asked the young man to come to see me.

He was a bright boy and I have no doubt at all but that his heart was in the right place. He was trying to help people, and when I asked him how he could harmonize his sense of Christian ethics with kissing a married woman, he had a ready answer. She was lonely and very unhappy; "I did not want her to feel rejected," was the way he put it. I have no doubt that he was sincere and that he was acting in perfect harmony with Fletcher's propositions. Yet, I could find no way to make this plain to the officials of the church, and it took a good deal of what I trust was godly manipulation to save the young man from a scandalous ending to his career. Is this what

146

Situation Ethics has in mind? I take my stand on the principle that all young preachers, and especially young counselors, had better be taught not to let their agape override a stodgy, moralistic law in their personal relations with married women in their congregations.

There are times when a law is a clumsy thing indeed. Every time the Methodist Church has passed a regulation to take care of some particular instance, I have the feeling it has been too bad. The law has the tendency to say that every man must wear the same size shoes and sleep in beds of the same length. But if a person takes the alternative, instead of coming out better he finds that he is worse off than before.

At the beginning of his book Joseph Fletcher quotes, and I suppose with approbation, these words from William Temple: "There is only one ultimate and invariable duty, and its formula is 'Thou shalt love thy neighbor as thyself.' How to do this is another question, but this is the whole of moral duty." [18] Quite so! But the significant part of this quotation from my point of view is the phrase: "How to do this is another question." Laws are attempts, oftentimes clumsy, to deal with this question of how to do it and man forgets them to his sorrow.

Fletcher's book fits the mood of our time and that is why it has had such widespread discussion. Over against this let me quote the secretary of Health, Education, and Welfare, John W. Gardner:

The image created by the beatniks and by most of their predecessors back to the nineteenth-century bohemians has led us to suppose that people of high originality are somehow lawless. But the only creative man is not an outlaw but a lawmaker. Every great creative performance since the initial one has been in some measure a bringing of order out of chaos. [19]

I look back to the apostle Paul as he wrestles with this problem in Romans. There were few men who found the law less adequate than Paul, but it is interesting that he never was willing to say it was unnecessary. Because we Christians are free from law we are not to sin and we are not to regard the law as evil. He can even go so far as to say, "So the law is holy, and the commandment is holy and just and good" (Rom. 7:12). The greatness of the New Testament is holding together things that must be part of any experience of wholeness; and the failure to appreciate this is the weakness of Fletcher's book. It shows a frightening unawareness of what is involved in social ethics and a lack of realism in considering what is necessary for men to live together in some kind of Christian social life.

The final impression that *Situation Ethics* makes upon me is of an arrogance so overpowering as to be almost unbelievable. Can any man announce that he is capable of deciding any question without help from his brethren? Is any person able to ignore tradition as if everything began with him at this particular moment? Can anyone subscribe to such an idea without being guilty of the pride which the Bible defines as the ultimate sin? Absolutes are for God alone and only the meek inherit the earth.

8

Situation Ethics Under Fire

*What replies can be given
to critics of situation ethics?*

JOSEPH FLETCHER

A storm over ethics? Yes, I suppose there is. And it seems that my little book *Situation Ethics* has proved to be a kind of catalyst or precipitant, having the effect that we get sometimes when a small plane flies high into the clouds to "seed" them with the right chemical, usually silver iodide, and manages to get the reluctant rain started down upon the parched earth. As the rainfall grows, new winds begin to blow; soon fresh and better rain will fall, hopefully leaving *Situation Ethics* far behind in the process.

The book was not written for biblically and theologically sophisticated readers. That much—its popular purpose—should be obvious. The main hope behind it was

Joseph Fletcher is professor of social ethics at Episcopal Theological School, Cambridge, Massachusetts.

to draw a wide range of nonprofessional people into the growing debate about "how to do" ethics. There is by now a reassuring pile of evidence that its primary purpose has been realized, and that the discussion has also spilled over into the more esoteric quarters where philosophical and theological specialists carry on their dialogue. The chapters in this present book are very substantial proof of how the debate flows back and forth between the two sectors—the popular and the professional. What has not yet been clearly enough understood is that the debate is *directly* only methodological, even though indirectly questions of "content" or "values" and "rules" are entailed and quite properly get drawn in as the debate probes around.

A recently published letter to the editor of *The Christian Century* provides us with an interesting parallel to the debate and argument in this volume. Let me quote it verbatim in order to preserve its flavor as well as its obvious bearing upon what we have experienced in the storm over ethics. Vernon Weiss writes of the reactions of four theologians to Bishop Robinson's *Honest to God*:

> In the course of their several lectures on the topic, they all made it clear that Robinson really didn't have anything to offer because (1) he didn't say anything new and (2) he didn't say it accurately as the various specialists would have liked. This was, of course, during the time when Robinson was selling like the proverbial hotcakes. In summing up the four lectures, the master of ceremonies . . . said to the lecturers, "Well, now, if what Robinson said has been old hat to you theologians for a generation, why hasn't the church heard it before?" [1]

Verbum sapienti sat est.

Much of what is said in the earlier chapters here about what is *not* in *Situation Ethics* is not necessarily anything I would disagree with. Obviously I left out far more than

I put in and to complain because it was not a "systematic" and "comprehensive" academic treatise misses the point, just as it is critically beside the point to deplore sharp and simple language of the sort we never use in professional books and journals. What, then, *is* the critical issue posed? Let me say plainly and starkly that the core question raised is, *Are there any moral principles, other than to do the most good possible, which oblige us in conscience at all times?* To this question situation ethics, which claims to be the appropriate method of the new morality and its relativism, gives a flat answer, *No*.

TAKE THE TEN COMMANDMENTS!

If we look straightforwardly at the decalogue, the Ten Commandments, we can unmistakably pose the issue as between the old and the new moralities. Situationists cannot and do not regard any of these ten ancient principles or rules or laws as always morally valid in practice; they have to be relativized by adding "ordinarily" in each case: we ought to tell the truth *ordinarily;* we ought not to kill *ordinarily;* we ought to respect our parents *ordinarily;* we ought not to steal *ordinarily*—but none of these rules is valid unless in each concrete situation it is "good" to follow it. And the criterion for "good" is whether our action is as loving as the situation allows.

If you can agree with what is said in the preceding paragraph, you are a practitioner of situation ethics. (There are plenty of *practical* situationists, but the new morality calls for being situational as a matter of belief and not just as a betrayal or compromise of the old morality— which is "legalistic" because it pretends to absolutize and universalize such "moral laws.") Bishop Kennedy and Fr.

Gleason, each in his own way, are quite definitely legalists. Whether President Bennett and Professor Smith are or are not is far from clear, just reading what they say here in this book. Professor Gardner and Professor Fackre are pretty plainly legalists by the test we are using. Professor Gustafson takes no issue with the core proposition of situation ethics, but his dislike of the term and his complaints about its use leave us a little unsure of just what his ethical method really is.

Indeed, the commonest reactions to the situationists' thesis are either "O shucks, we are all situationists, of course; but do you have to say it out so raw and bald like?" or "You don't *really* mean what you say; you just want to shock us and make us think." But situationism is indeed relativistic, it does actually deny all "eternal" or "absolute" rules of conduct. Its "clarity about charity" may, for reasons not hard to appreciate, shock old-style moralists with their legalism and moralism, but it means just what it says while eagerly welcoming any fresh thinking people are willing to do.

William James's remark about the reception of pragmatism applies here too. First it was met with the retort, "Nonsense. Ridiculous. It's perfectly absurd—or wicked." The next line of resistance was, "It's obvious, a platitude. Not important." Finally it takes the form, "Very true. Essential. That's what I've been saying all along." Situation ethics, as the method theory of the new morality, does not claim that it is new in the sense of being novel or unprecedented. But the vigorous debate going on these days shows that a breakthrough has occurred—a breakthrough that should be recognized in a broader context, as a companion piece to the new theology and the new evangelism which reflect the pluralism and empiricism and relativism of "mature men" in the modern age. It gives up the classical metaphysical apparatus of ethical a prioris and ontologically "grounded" axioms.

I feel I should apologize for the first person singular format which this chapter is taking, but it cannot be helped because so much of our book is a sharp examination of *Situation Ethics* and of the methodology I advocate. It does not often happen that a little volume of 175 pages stirs up so much analysis by such a wide range of big and little critics, pro and con. At least the use of first person references gives this discussion considerable human warmth and my book provides a documentary focus. It is abundantly plain that the contributors to this symposium are taking the issues posed in a serious way. In some cases they correctly discern the issues and in other cases they are falsely or even wildly off the mark. Altogether it is a useful contribution to the continuing and deepening debate about how to do ethics.

Even in Christian circles the debate may be moving far more rapidly than most people suppose. To cite developments in only one quarter, the Roman Catholic Church, we should all be aware of such pressure gauges as two recently published essays having a decidedly pro-situational direction in them. One is a quite professional paper read by Robert O. Johann, S.J., at the University of Kansas, "Love and Justice," in which Fr. Johann asserts most equably, "The ultimate norm in the moral realm and *its only absolute law* is thus the law of intelligent responsiveness." He adds that the precepts of code morality (such as the Ten Commandments?) "can serve as guidelines in the making of moral decisions" but they "cannot be finally decisive in our moral choices." [2]

The other essay is by Bishop Francis Simons, elaborating an intervention he made at the Second Vatican Council, in which he says quite directly, "Whenever the good of mankind demands that the general rule or commandment should not apply, it does not apply. This evident consequence gives us an easy solution of certain moral problems which have bedeviled moral theologians who believe in the absoluteness of the commandments." Although he hedges explicitly that his essay is not "an exercise in situation ethics," he then goes on to stipulate as elastic and changeable eight once-supposed "precepts of the natural law" (*mirabile dictu*): truth-telling, killing, abortion, suicide, sterilization, masturbation, divorce and remarriage, and artificial insemination.[3]

Johann and Simons are much farther down the road than is Bernard Häring, C.SS.R., yet even he is trying in his gentle and melioristic fashion to find an advance post for discourse with situationists. Hence in his recent *Toward a Christian Moral Theology* (an arresting title), he declares that as far as "positive" law is concerned, whether civil or ecclesiastical, moral rules can be changed or disregarded; that is, relativized. "There is," he says, "full agreement on this point between Catholic theologians and the proponents of situation ethics."[4] But not so, he holds, when it comes to "natural" moral laws—among which he would include the Ten Commandments. Indeed, the Commandments get the "double whammy" because he would also agree with Protestant (old) moralists that they are *revealed* laws as well as natural.

To this doctrine of "given" goodness, revealed and/or discerned "in the nature of things," situationists retort, "All moral laws are relative, finite, contingent—be they positive, natural, revealed, or whatnot." Yet one senses in this "storm over ethics" that Roman Catholic Christians

with their worn-out "old" casuistry might more easily in-
corporate situation-method's neo-casuistry than old-mo-
rality Protestants can with their fiat-absolutisms, if only
they can find a way to get rid of "deontology" by "de-
ontologizing" their norms and values. There is a basic
partnership between deontology or law ethics and ontology as in the ethical realism of Thomist metaphysics. Can
that partnership be dissolved?

Now let me "talk" in open forum with each of the
writers whose criticisms are included in this book. With
the exception of Fr. Gleason's chapter they were all written as "statements" in the debate as it has shaped up in
the last year—a very up-to-date exchange. Out of this
dialogue, we may hope, further discourse and rhetoric
will manage to pinpoint and crystallize the determinative
questions more carefully than any of us has succeeded in
doing thus far and will do so more constructively and
with more generosity than some have shown.

BENNETT

It is flogging a docetic horse to treat the problem as one
of "context *versus* principles." That issue only arises as
between moralists who are impromptu, unprincipled, and
spontaneous in their ethical method—for example, ancient antinomians and modern existentialists—*and all the
rest of us.* Whether we are legalists who absolutize and
universalize some norms and rules, or situationists who
have norms and rules but relativize and empiricize them
all, we are as such united against the spontaneists. Using
categories or labels familiar in philo-theological rhetoric,
legalists hold a "pure *rules*-ethics," spontaneists or extem-
porists favor a "pure *act*-ethics," and situationists are in

a mediating position—which may be seen either as "*modified* rules-ethics" or as "modified act-ethics." The true issue is over whether we can absolutize, universalize, and "finalize" any normative principle: legalists say Yes, situationists say No. *But both are agreed that both context or situation and principles or moral generalizations ("summary rules") are needed in ethical judgment.* (Situationists practice "principled relativism.")

In Christian ethics Bultmann is indeed an existentialist, as he has all along been at great pains to make quite clear. As such he proposes a nonrational and intuitive-inspirationist (which?) theory or method of ethical decision-making in situ. Neither principle-absolutizers (legalists) nor principle-relativizers (situationists) can follow Bultmann's impulsive and subjective method of making judgments.[5]

Most of us do not trust too much to Joseph Sittler's gull-swoop of conscience, as President Bennett rightly remarks.[6] But neither, in fact, did Barth or Bonhoeffer trust it. This method, which Bishop Robinson calls "homing" intuitively on a right decision, and which he unfortunately embraces as a "built-in moral compass," [7] is not situational but spontaneous or extemporist or existential or transrational. What Bennett calls "criteria" I have called general principles which illuminate situations as guidelines, but (as I would hold, and maybe Bennett too) without necessarily predetermining our actions.

As a situationist and "love monist" I can applaud Bennett's saying that what is required is "love as it seeks knowledge concerning the needs of the community of neighbors," even though I have preferred to say "justice is love using its head" and "love seeks the most good possible for the most neighbors possible." And when he insists that love seeking the good of the neighbors "must be guided by norms," my only comment is that I, at least, have never said anything different. The main point is that I would be careful to add, "We are never to be bound in any situation by our norms." This is what a responsible ethics, an ethics of response, situation ethics, holds to.

It seems to me that there is no substantial issue as between Bennett's published view and situationism's.

GUSTAFSON

Yes. The discriminating questions are: (1) How do we make judgments (the methodological question with which I have been wrestling), and (2) by what norms? But the real difference between my method and Paul Ramsey's is not, as Professor Gustafson suggests at one point, the difference between my being an "act agapist" and Ramsey's being a "rule agapist." This is much too simple. Gustafson moves on later and more perceptively to recognize that both Ramsey and I are in our methods "modified." (This is a term, by the way, which was introduced into the present rhetoric by Frankena to moderate "act utilitarianism," but it can be used—I suggest that we do so—for *any* kind of ethic when it is polarized into "rule" and "act" forms—or, as I have preferred to label them, "legalist" and "extemporist." Extending Frankena's language we can call situation ethics "modified rule-agapism." [8]

It is to be noted, of course, that my method stresses the act (that is, the act-in-the-situation), whereas Ramsey's stresses the "principles" or moral generalizations and value propositions which are called into play and reference. Yet both of us, Ramsey and I, are agreed in reject-

157

ing the polarized either-or choice of ethical methods; that is, we both modify them. Even though Ramsey speaks of in-principled love, he does not absolutize love's principles. (After all, he couldn't do so and still follow the relativistic line he does; for example, in connection with the ethics of just war and revolution.[9])

It is a pity to waste time or space over Gustafson's distractive quarreling. Surely I do not "seem" to want to eliminate bad conscience; not once but twice I have referred in print to Schweitzer's warning that a good conscience is the devil's invention. The charge that I have an "unwarranted confidence in the directing and informing power of love" (an interesting complaint to be brought by a *Christian* moralist) is significantly unsupported by any chapter and verse. It is an amazing charge in view of the far more common complaint to just the opposite effect —that I treat love as coldly rational and allow no place for inspiration or guidance in decision-making. However, there is at least a first-order issue here. Gustafson's term love monism is meant pejoratively ("pluralism" is the "in" word these days), but it pinpoints a crucial question— whether the love of Christian ethics, as a formal principle, can provide the normative criteria needed for ethical judgment. For in some real sense situation ethics is indeed a version of love monism—or, even phrasier, "monistic agapism."

There is no lack of fit between my methodological thesis and a delineation of love's meaning such as H. Richard Niebuhr's in *The Purpose of the Church and Its Ministry.*[10] Situationists hail with delight his conceptual breakdown of the formal principle of love (he calls its increase "the goal of the church") into such categories as rejoicing in the neighbor, gratitude to him, reverence for him, and loyalty to him. But surely it is plain that these "normatives" are no closer to operational terms or to the nuts and bolts language of situational decision-making than agape is.

Gustafson speaks of my remarks about "happiness," in connection with which I cite Aristotle, as if this makes Aristotle and me hedonists. He does so, moreover, without any reference to my repudiation of that and similar terms (see *Situation Ethics,* pp. 96-97). He then moves on to an accusation that I have dropped or ignored obligation, duty, self-denial, social issues, concern for others, repentance. What is needed to demonstrate the puzzling and totally unexpected animus here, other than to refer the careful reader to *Situation Ethics,* to pages 27, 60, 74, 82, 95, 100, 144, and 157 on obligation and duty; to 79, 82, 88, 91, 105, and especially 110-14 on self-denial; to 50, 83, the whole of chapter 5, especially 99-102, on social issues and concern for others, as well as references to anarchism, capital punishment, civil rights, communism, divorce, gambling, political assassination, racism, securities trading, guerrilla warfare, Marxism, pacifism, revolution, and nuclear war; to 116, 124 (where the *real* issue is posed); and 152 on repentance, sin, and forgiveness. Yet Gustafson is getting at something on the last score—repentance. Situation ethics clearly delimits our grounds for remorse as distinct from regret! Professor Gardner's analysis of the issue is much more perceptive and clarifying, especially in noting that while my thesis has a place for personal sin in the classical sense it has none for "original" sin. The latter is consciously and deliberately discarded. (As archaic and semantically confused—not the condition of self-centeredness, of course, but the notion that the *fact* is an ought-factor, a "sin.")

In the last analysis we must acknowledge—nay, profess
—that *Christian* situation ethics is indeed "love monism"
compared to any ethics in which agape is "included" as
only one normative criterion or standard along with or
among others.

GARDNER

After all, as Professor Gardner says, "situation ethics" is
a thesis about method. He is right to insist that normative
principles are of great importance, however much the
situationist may relativize them in practice. It is therefore
interesting that he excites himself into saying that I show
a "rejection of law."

Gardner complains that I have lumped too wide a range
of moralists under the umbrella of situationism. Possibly
he is right. I simply used the list given by Gustafson,
which included Gustafson himself.[11] Yet I agree with the
view that the "umbrella" is too wide in the sense that
there are discernible and even important differences of
emphasis between them, even though all are agreed (at
least on the surface, pro forma) as to the relativity of normative principles. And certainly none of them would be
either unprincipled, on the one hand, or on the other
committed to absolutes whether of the natural or scrip-
tural orders.

Contrary to Gardner's way of seeing it, there is no contradiction in saying that although classical Christian ethics has been legalistic, most men (including Christians)
have been situationists in practice. My point is, to be
blunt about it, that they have been what Salinger's
Holden Caulfield called phonies—talking one line, following another. This is the basic hypocrisy of the old

morality. Situation ethics is infinitely more honest, less given to self-deceiving rhetoric about "principles." Even the idolatry of Stephen Decatur's "my country right or wrong" is preferable to the old morality's "my principles are God's, always right, never wrong."

I can only respond to Clinton Gardner, with dogged patience and persistence, that I do *not* "equate" love and justice. I identify them, conflate them, make them one and the same thing. Love does not equal justice, it *is* justice; and vice versa. They are not two different things closely related or of equal force; they are one thing without variance or alternation or opposition of the same. It is this part of *Situation Ethics* (chapter 5) which appears more and more vital to an understanding of love as it is conceived in the Christian situationist's theoretical apparatus.

Gardner understands me correctly on one point. I do not, certainly do not, follow Brunner's "orders," nor for that matter Luther's or the Catholic version, nor Bonhoeffer's "mandates." I regard them as covert forms of the classical natural law doctrine—as "values" which are supposed to be given ontologically in objective reality or in the "very nature of things" created ex nihilo. On the contrary, the new morality follows the call to de-Hellenize or de-ontologize our ethics as well as our doctrine. This is the demand of the new morality, as it is of the new theology—as uttered, for example, by Bishop Pike and Professor Leslie Dewart.[12] There are lots of nominalists or non-realists in the woods these days.

It is impossible, of course, to know what it means to charge me with being "too" exclusively christological, but in any case Gardner is quite right that my version of theological ethics moves from Christology to theology, not vice versa. He appears to want it the other way, without showing why or how it affects the method-question in Christian ethics. (I suspect he is unhappy about it for the reason suggested above. Metaphysical theism fits his ontological presuppositions better.) But, in any case, here is a vital issue in Christian ethics and he has done well to "zero" in on it. He may seem to some to suspect me of being a crypto-Marcionite, to judge by his unassailable remarks about the Old Testament being part of the Bible, but while this is a puzzling section of his criticism, and rather gratuitous as it stands, his concern with the theology at stake is much to the point.

Another odd bit is his statement "He assumes that the only usage of law is prescriptive; hence, he ignores its illuminative role. . . ." Actually, I have been saying all along that principles or laws or general rules *are,* as I myself describe them, "illuminators." Law is a good thing when it serves love's purpose—but love is boss, not law. We all know Luther's *Book of Concord* and his "uses of the law," so close to Calvin's later on, and I made this quite clear in *Situation Ethics* (p. 62) by a direct quotation from Luther calling law "a proof of love" while still asserting we must "suspend the law" when it injures the neighbor (Luther's language, not mine).

Gardner's major discontents are: (1) I am too christological, (2) too individualistic, and (3) too nonhistorical or discontinuous, too much given to an "ahistorical present." But I don't know what "too" means. It seems to be a mood rather than critical objection. I doubt if he would think me "too" New Testamentish if the book had been tailored, as it was not, as an exercise in biblical study (as *his* was). As to his second complaint, there is simply no ground for it at all. As in Gustafson's case, it is pure eisegesis. The fact that the complaint is made at all is proof that even trained people are vulnerable to the errors of arguing from silence. I put it this way because my book is a methodological treatise, not a normative study of either interpersonal or social ethics. Even so I tried to protect Gardner and Gustafson from their mistake by references to nearly thirty social questions (more than interpersonal ones) to show that the *method* applies to both. On his third score, he would have been more telling critically if he had said that situationism is better served by a more integrative definition of the situation than I gave it. It should go without saying that a situationist could have as much historical insight as anybody; the past is part of the data. But as some have pointed out to me, the book should have done more to indicate that there is usually a "network of situations" to be considered rather than just *the* situation. This is true and a fair criticism. A narrow scope of "situation" would falsify.

FACKRE

In a lively beginning Professor Fackre uses a *reductio ad absurdum* case (his family's household chores) to show that "situationism is a perfectly legitimate position if it is used itself situationally." Good. *Concerto!* No debate. (Does he think there is?)

He says, "The problem is not solved simply by affirming that neighbor-love is our absolute." Very few problems of conscience are solved *simply*—even when the method is that of prefabricating legalism. Traditional casuistry with its "perplexity" and "doubt" about moral law is testimony to the complexity, not the simplicity, even of legalistic morality. Evidently Fackre means that we have to

163

weigh up the facts in the situation or in the network of situations. Good. *Concerto!* No debate. (Does he think there is?)

"We need to set bounds to the chaos and injustice that irresponsible people can inflict on society—hence the need for laws." Good. *Concerto!* No debate. (Does Fackre think there is?)

"To transcend law, however, is not to dissolve it, any more than the presence of the New Testament abolishes the significance of the Old." Right. Let's have the law, let's be ready to transcend it if love requires. Good. *Concerto!* No debate. (Is Fackre charging love-ethics with being Marcionite, or only insinuating it, or what?)

When he speaks of situation ethics as "playing it by ear" he has obviously confused it with extemporism and the existentialists' approach. Enough said, *supra.*

It is not very easy to penetrate and fix the thought in Fackre's article. For example, is he saying that situation ethics as such is "angelism," or only that the adventuristic sex-is-fun ethos is angelistic? We could certainly agree in the latter case, but if he means the former he is manifestly burlesqueing the problem. Perhaps the difficulty here lies in Fackre's preoccupation with sex rather than with the deeper and more critical ethical questions at stake.

SMITH

Professor Smith is probably on good ground in finding that situation ethics is closer than classical Christian ethics and moral theology to moral autonomy theories. But we must not overlook the point that "moral autonomy" in philosophical discourse is of two kinds, one referring to the autonomy of norms (they are not given or prede-

164

termined or chosen *for* the moral agent, not "handed down" or "revealed" or "self-evident"), the other referring to the autonomy of the moral agent himself (not a creature of imposed norms and values, nor of necessarily causal conduct, but responsible and free to decide for or against obedience). It is the latter kind of autonomy, the autonomy of the agent, which fits situation ethics at least approximately. If the situationist is a Christian his norms are not his own, he does not choose them for himself by any means, as if he were not part of a loyalty and heritage —but *he* has to decide in every situation whether he will follow them or not.

Needless to say, we should all appreciate Smith's characterization of legalism and extemporism, the two "outside" ethical strategies (which he prefers to call models). He does them with grace and knowledge. But his claim that I have a big place for teleology (goal orientation) and little or none for deontology (duty orientation) would lose any significance if he had explained to his readers how I showed that neither of these traditional classifications in philosophical ethics really excludes the other or represents a truly discrete class. For a Christian, for example, the goal is to obey God's command to love the neighbor and his duty is to seek to be loving—or, in H. Richard Niebuhr's terms, to "increase love." The analytic and descriptive habits of the old morality only partially work in dealing with the new situationist strategy, and traditional categories are now more easily seen to be of little relevance and adequacy.

To take another example from Smith's treatment, it is hard to recognize oneself as a "Platonist" merely because he takes seriously the Johannine faith that God is love and that man is not God. It is equally difficult to see oneself as somehow ethereally hovering over a situation, untouched or uninvolved in it, simply because I "face" situations calling for decisions. One wonders, does Smith enjoy some other alternative to trying to look at what calls out for action and then, even though involved oneself by the very fact of being called to act, acting? If he does, he escapes the uneasy and uncomfortable problem of being both free and "engaged," and his lot is a happier one than mine and most men's.

If I may be quite plainspoken, Smith's desire to show that I only "suggest" that agape is not possible for man is a perverse desire. This view of man as agapeic in deed but not in being is not a puddle of illogic into which I have slipped carelessly. On the contrary, I explicitly *declare* it. The point is that only *God* is love, yet as the apostle Paul said so often we human beings can find in God's being (love, made manifest in Jesus) an example of *how we are to do*. But it is certainly not a manifestation of what or whom we are to *be!* After all, if we are to take theology seriously in Christian ethics, what else can be said about the matter? Smith misconstrues the position by saying it is meaningless to ask us to imitate God or Christ, "owing to man's incapacity for the love of which only God is capable." All along I have said that man is capable of *responding* to God's love, however imperfectly —yet only God *is* love. Smith should have no difficulty in grasping the conventional philosophical distinction between properties and predicates.

Again, I am at a loss to find where or how I have ever used, in this last book or any earlier one—have, that is, *ever* said anything even remotely like Smith's reconstruction of my position on the nature of the good. He says that "whereas medievalists [surely he means nominalists] argued that good is good because God wills it, Fletcher argues that man makes this decision." Does he mean that I hold that men decide for God what God wills or should will—which is love? That would be nonsensical. The clear alternative to the nonsensical reading of Smith's statement would be that men have to decide for themselves what the loving will of God, known in principle by faith, can and shall mean in any concrete situation. What other alternative is there? This is, of course, what I have been saying plainly and definitely. Am I utterly and suddenly bereft of basic philosophical acumen? This is what he seems to be saying.

Smith is not quite correct to find "it has not been argued before" that a loving act made necessary because of the situation, even though it violates a rule, is "positively" good. This is exactly what a practical adoption of ethical relativism entails, as all modern ethicists beginning with Edward Westermarck have held, and I embrace it deliberately and wittingly. Smith's position requires him to establish what he has not established, either the case historically for his "not . . . before" (Westermarck is only one obvious refutation) or a convincing conceptualization of "positively" which discredits and alienates all relativists.

Situationism is, as Smith recognizes, a corrective of legalism and extemporism. But he simply does not *like* the philosophical implications. I can understand this temper and feel some sympathy for his turnings and twistings, but they are after all only the heartburn of the old morality. Furthermore, I applaud his insistence on the need for creative risk-taking. As a situationist I must. But quite obviously he experiences the classical and conventional difficulties with what he and John Dourley think of as man's progressive humanization. It both attracts and frightens them. But this is what situation ethics knowingly and bravely embraces, with all of the relativism and moral humility and *pecca fortiter* of finite humanity.

GLEASON

Fr. Gleason's paper, though written before the rise of the present debate, provides a fine, learned, and carefully expounded anti-situationist essay.

It suffers, as does so much Roman Catholic writing on the subject, from the failure to perceive how situation ethics is a mediating position between ethical absolutism and the unprincipled ethics of existentialism. Gleason confuses situationism with the spontaneist or antinomian method of doing ethics. Nevertheless, much of what he says about existentialist ethics fits situation ethics too. It is worth reading carefully for that reason, among others.

He also confuses the "personalism" of an ethics which gives first order value to persons with the "personal" (self-authenticating) decision-making of the I-centered antinomians. Both of these postures are opposed to "juridical" and "manualistic" ethics, but the Christian situationist is a personalist only in the first sense, not in the second. This confusion is what leads Gleason to speak of situationists as those who "rely heavily" on "movements of spirits" rather than upon syllogistic (read "logical") reasoning, but this applies actually only to the antinomians and not to situationists. They, situationists, are not "subjectivists," as he thinks.

Gleason's essay is a superior example of the classical Catholic treatment of theological ethics, firmly based in the official "line" but generous to counter considerations.

He is correct to find that the new morality is at bottom nominalist rather than realist, Occamist or Scotist rather than Thomist in its metaethical theory of value and being. But it would not be to the point to say that there is no possible conflict between law and charity (love) if both are accepted. For the situationist insists that while they are not always or even ordinarily in conflict, *sometimes they are!* And in such situations, we contend, a law such as one of the second tablet of the Ten Commandments must be set aside. Yes, even one of the laws of the decalogue. This is what Fr. Gleason cannot accept. There is a much sharper and spikier issue at stake than his gentle manner will allow to be openly tested.

Yet he comes finally close to the bone and marrow when he says flatly that some actions, such as lying, "are always and in every circumstance wrong." There it is in black and white. There is the nettle, straightly grasped.

I will repeat what I have said elsewhere about this essay of his, that when he calls love a "noble" motive but not the exclusive one for Christians he is wrong. Agape is not just one among other normative principles, as Gleason holds—and as Gustafson implies by the label "love monism."

Finally, Gleason need not approach things so obliquely by saying that "no doubt" situationism is relativistic "at least in its extreme forms." It is relativistic in any form. There is no need to appear to deduce or adduce or infer the relativism of situation ethics. Its exponents now plainly declare it to be so. They accept fully his statement of situationism, that "while admitting the validity of general principles, it does not admit that they are ultimate or absolute." They use principles all right, but they are not used by them. Moral principles were made for men, not men for moral principles. That is situation ethics in a nut-shell.

In spite of his false start by dragging "heresy" in (who is free of that vintage concept's dour stare these days?), I find it hard to wrestle with an essay which begins by citing Chesterton, for he is high on my list too. It shows that we, Bishop Kennedy and I, are near contemporaries.

Kennedy holds that we have to have law because it is a mistake to let people decide for themselves what is good. But there is hardly any escape from that decision, anyway. Even in a legalistic ethos people have to decide that law in general is to be obeyed and a particular law in every situation. We don't really escape decision by law talk. As I emphasized in *Situation Ethics,* to be alive is to be deciding.

I would prefer to deal with a straightforward legalist, such as Kennedy professes to be. They are not very numerous; most of the critics of situation ethics are far less candid than he. Yet, even so, I am appalled by his argument from the pressures of Methodist church government to the need for dropping a man (minister) who is divorced *even though he will be restored later.* And it is clearly a double standard of morality that he is recommending, because the Methodists do not apply that particular form of legalism to their lay members. The same is true of his defense of laws against abortion and euthanasia, at the same time that he says he has no doubt that such things are sometimes *right.*

The bishop has good reason to suggest, as previously

170

noted, that a basic issue is ethical ontology—or, as he expresses it, "There are written into the very nature of things certain principles. . . ." This is the classical natural law doctrine. Situationists, at least of my own stamp, do most certainly discard that ancient bit of metaphysics and speculation. It poses unquestionably a crucial issue for all Catholics and many Protestants, in the line of the old morality. But Kennedy does not clarify the issues merely by reasserting the doctrine.

He says that I absolutize love, which indeed I do, and that I eliminate any place for law, which I most certainly and clearly do not do. It is an odd and I suspect revealing myopia. He can read, but he cannot read situation ethics. But how can this common misreading be got rid of? Kennedy recognized at the outset of his criticism that I have a place for moral laws as general principles. What he means at the end, therefore, when he says that I "eliminate" law, is that I refuse to absolutize normative principles in the same way I absolutize love. We cannot absolutize both, and the New Testament makes it perfectly clear which of them is to be absolute!

The story about the silly young Methodist minister's kissing the "lonely" and "unhappy" married woman is dirty pool in serious debate. And so with the questions in Kennedy's closing paragraph. He obviously means to imply that I wouldn't *dare* to answer them in the negative— but of course I do.

SOMETHING TO GO ON

The debate is just getting well started. There will be more and better to come and all of us, whichever side we

171

stand on, will get new insight and a clearer grasp of the issues. In a serious and courteous review, John G. Milhaven, S.J., poses an excellent list of questions or issues as between the old morality and the thesis of situation ethics, and their quiet, unpretentious formulation makes them promising questions with which to continue examining the merits of the controversy, pro and con.[13] He allows that *Situation Ethics* may be "too popular in tone" for some, "too pedantic" for others, yet "a welcome and substantial contribution" which, for the old moralists of both Catholic and Protestant ethics, "will hasten the review of the process whereby the absolutes are determined."

Let us all, whatever method of doing ethics we may advocate, continue to ponder Fr. Milhaven's seven questions. Situationists can profit by exploring them, just as much as their opponents.

1. *Are* there no absolutes but love alone?
2. What do maxims (as distinct from laws) *tell* people?
3. *How* do they illuminate a problem?
4. How are they adduced from *experience?*
5. What determines whether an action *is* loving?
6. *What* does love strive to bring about?
7. Is there *a hierarchy of "goods"* in love's "goodwill"?

We need a lot more of the best criticism we can get. As Professor Cross says, ending a long and very probing review of my book in the *Anglican Theological Review,* situation ethics "embodies the promise of a novel, relevant, and penetrating approach to the perplexing and sor-

172

did moral issues of these disturbed times. . . . As it fulfills this role of criticism and estimation, it will prove its casuistical usefulness and vindicate its vocation as a new incentive in moral thought." [14]

Notes

CHAPTER 1

1. This chapter is a revision of the presidential address delivered in 1961 to the American Society of Christian Social Ethics. It formed the basis of the critical discussion of the author's view in Paul Lehmann, *Ethics in a Christian Context* (New York: Harper & Row, 1963), pp. 148-54. A few paragraphs have been added to the address and some of the illustrations have been modified to bring them up to date, but the main argument that Professor Lehmann criticizes is preserved. The author has also added a few references to Professor Lehmann's thought, which may help to bring out the difference between the two viewpoints.

2. Thomas C. Oden, *Radical Obedience: The Ethics of Rudolph Bultmann* (Philadelphia: Westminster Press, 1964), p. 35.

3. *Ibid.*, p. 145.

4. Karl Barth, *Against the Stream* (Naperville, Ill.: Alec R. Allenson, Inc., 1954), p. 114.

5. Karl Barth, *Church Dogmatics*, eds. G. W. Bromiley and T. F. Torrance (Edinburgh: T. & T. Clark, 1936-ca. 1962), II/2, 661 ff.

6. Karl Barth, *Community, State, and Church* (New York: Doubleday, 1960), pp. 149-89.

7. *Ibid.*, p. 42.

8. *Ibid.*, p. 43.

9. Barth, *Church Dogmatics*, III/4, 436.

10. Dietrich Bonhoeffer, *Ethics*, ed. Eberhard Bethge (New York: Macmillan, 1955), p. 23.

11. *Ibid.*, p. 126.

12. *Ibid.*, pp. 131 ff.

13. *Ibid.*, p. 131 n.

14. *Ibid.*, pp. 305 f.

15. Lehmann, *op. cit.*, p. 152.

16. Cf. Edmond Cahn, *The Sense of Injustice* (Bloomington: Indiana University Press, 1964).

17. Joseph Fletcher, *Situation Ethics: The New Morality* (Philadelphia: Westminster Press, 1966), p. 26.

18. Cf. chapter 2, "Love Monism."

19. Amos Wilder refers to a significant statement made by Professor Iwand of Bonn, one of the pillars of the Confessing Church in Germany, to the effect that "if evangelical churches of Germany had been clearer in their own thinking about what a state could and could not do and what a Christian as a citizen could and could not permit, the assumption of power by national socialism would have been more effectively resisted." Cf. Amos Wilder, "Kerygma, Eschatology, and Social Ethics," *The Background of the New Testament and Its Eschatology*, eds. W. D. Davies and D. Daube (New York: Cambridge University Press, 1964). This is an excellent example of the importance of bringing something more than a religious commitment without relevant ethical content to the situation.

CHAPTER 2

1. James M. Gustafson, "Context Versus Principles: A Misplaced Debate in Christian Ethics," *New Theology No. 3*, eds. Martin E. Marty and Dean G. Peerman (New York: Macmillan, 1966), pp. 69-102.

2. Joseph Fletcher, *Situation Ethics: The New Morality* (Philadelphia: Westminster Press, 1966), p. 95.

3. H. Richard Niebuhr, *The Purpose of the Church and Its Ministry* (New York: Harper & Bros., 1956), pp. 35 f.

4. Paul Ramsey, *Deeds and Rules in Christian Ethics* ("Scottish Journal of Theology Occasional Papers," No. 11 [Edinburgh: Oliver and Boyd, 1965]), p. 35, quoting H. A. Williams, "Theology and Self-Awareness," *Soundings*, ed. A. R. Vidler (New York: Cambridge University Press, 1962), p. 82.

CHAPTER 3

1. George Woods, "Situational Ethics," *Christian Ethics and Contemporary Philosophy*, ed. Ian T. Ramsey (New York: Macmillan, 1966), p. 339.

2. Cf., for example, John A. T. Robinson, *Christian Morals Today* (Philadelphia: Westminster Press, 1964); and James M. Gustafson, "Context Versus Principles: A Misplaced Debate in Christian Ethics," *Harvard Theological Review*, LVIII, 2 (April, 1965), 171-202.

3. Joseph Fletcher, *Situation Ethics: The New Morality* (Philadelphia: Westminster Press, 1966), pp. 11, 13.

4. *Ibid.*, p. 40.

5. *Ibid.*, p. 18.

6. *Ibid.*

7. *Ibid.*, p. 36.

8. *Ibid.*, p. 147.

9. *Ibid.*

10. Emil Brunner, *Justice and the Social Order*, trans. Mary Hottinger (London: Lutterworth Press, 1945).

11. Emil Brunner, *The Divine Imperative*, trans. Olive Wyon (Philadelphia: Westminster Press, 1947).

12. Fletcher, *op. cit.*, p. 79.

13. *Ibid.*, p. 103.

14. *Ibid.*, p. 134.

15. *Ibid.*, p. 108.

16. Cf., for example, H. Richard Niebuhr, *Christ and Culture* (New York: Harper & Bros., 1951), pp. 15-19. Cf. Anders Nygren, *Agape and Eros* (London: Society for Promoting Christian Knowledge, 1953); cf. also Paul Tillich, *Love, Power, and Justice* (New York: Oxford University Press, 1954).

17. Fletcher, *op. cit.*, pp. 110-14.

18. Cf. Tillich, *op. cit.*, pp. 6, 33 f. For a fuller discussion of the author's own analysis of this problem, cf. E. Clinton Gardner, *Biblical Faith and Social Ethics* (New York: Harper & Bros., 1960), pp. 174-86.

19. Fletcher, *op. cit.*, p. 95.

20. *Ibid.*

21. *Ibid.*, p. 96.

22. *Ibid.*, p. 115.

23. *Ibid.*, p. 61.

24. *Ibid.*, p. 62.

25. *Ibid.*, p. 124.

26. *Ibid.*, pp. 135 **f.**

27. *Ibid.*, p. 136.

28. *Ibid.*, p. 152.

29. *Ibid.*, p. 45.

30. *Ibid.*

31. *Ibid.*, p. 64.

32. *Ibid.*, p. 55.

33. *Ibid.*

34. *Ibid.*, p. 36.

35. *Ibid.*, p. 140.

36. *Ibid.*, p. 155.
37. *Ibid.*, p. 157.
38. *Ibid.*
39. *Ibid.*
40. For a fuller development of the interpretation of Christian ethics upon which the present essay rests, cf. Gardner, *Biblical Faith and Social Ethics*. The author has been deeply influenced in his understanding of Christian ethics by his former mentor, the late Prof. H. Richard Niebuhr. For a fuller treatment of the germinal ideas reflected in this portion of the essay, cf. H. Richard Niebuhr's *Christ and Culture* (New York: Harper & Bros., 1951), *Radical Monotheism and Western Culture* (New York: Harper & Bros., 1960), and *The Responsible Self* (New York: Harper & Row, 1963).
41. Fletcher, *op. cit.*, p. 155.
42. Compare John C. Bennett (ed.), *Christian Social Ethics in a Changing World* (New York: Association Press, 1966). Note especially the essays by William H. Lazareth, H. D. Wendland, and John C. Bennett. Cf. also Paul Ramsey's incisive discussion of the role of law in Christian ethics in his *Deeds and Rules in Christian Ethics* ("Scottish Journal of Theology Occasional Papers," No. 11 [Edinburgh: Oliver and Boyd, 1965]).
43. H. Richard Niebuhr, "The Center of Value," *Radical Monotheism and Western Culture*, p. 107.
44. Cf. *ibid.*, p. 103.
45. Fletcher, *op. cit.*, p. 45.
46. Cf. Reinhold Niebuhr, *The Nature and Destiny of Man* (New York: Charles Scribner's Sons, 1943), II, 246 ff.
47. Cf. G. Ernest Wright, "The Faith of Israel," *The Interpreter's Bible* (Nashville: Abingdon Press, 1952), I, 389.
48. Cf. H. Richard Niebuhr, *Christ and Culture*, chap. 2.
49. *Ibid.*, pp. 241 ff.
50. Cf. Genesis 2:24; Mark 10:6-9.
51. For a probing analysis of this dimension of the moral situation, cf. H. Richard Niebuhr, *The Responsible Self*, pp. 90-107.

CHAPTER 4

1. Tom Wolfe, "Speaking Out: Down with Sin!" *The Saturday Evening Post* (June 19, 1965), pp. 12 ff.
2. This chapter is a revision of an article that appeared in *Theology and Life*, VIII, 4 (Winter, 1965), 251-66.

The fact that the phrase new morality is usually interpreted as new *sex* morality reveals our preoccupation with the private sector and gives force to the allegation that many today are in retreat from the great public issues of morality: war and peace, poverty, race. The attempt by some to restate the meaning of obscenity so as to include the public as well as the private arenas of morality is a wholesome corrective to this, as is the effort to place the question of sex in the context of the more wide-ranging public issues. In order to make contact with popular usage, and in recognition of the importance of sex ethics in its own right, I do confine my discussion of the new morality here to the issues raised by the new sex morality.

3. Harvey Cox, "*Playboy*'s Doctrine of Male," *Christianity and Crisis*, XXL, 6 (April 17, 1961), 56-60, and available in reprint. Essentially the same treatment can be found in Harvey Cox, *The Secular City* (New York: Macmillan, 1965), pp. 199-204.

4. Joseph Fletcher quoted in James L. Hofford, "Harvard Conference on the 'New Morality,'" *The Christian Century*, LXXXII, 13 (March 31, 1965), 409.

5. Joseph Fletcher, *Situation Ethics: The New Morality* (Philadelphia: Westminster Press, 1966), pp. 29 f., 45, 142 f.

6. *Time*, LXXXV, 10 (March 5, 1965), 44.

7. Cf. the exegetical discussion in Lindsay Dewar, *Moral Theology in the Modern World* (London: A. R. Mowbray & Co., Ltd., 1964), pp. 51 ff.

8. Even this is an oversimplification, for because of man's creaturely rootedness in social, economic, and political institutions, changes in the latter structures do influence readiness for ideational growth.

9. Roger Mehl, *Society and Love*, trans. James H. Farley (Philadelphia: Westminster Press, 1964), p. 211.

CHAPTER 5

1. James Daane, "Love Without Law," *Christianity Today* (October 8, 1965), p. 33.

2. Cf. Emil Brunner, *The Divine Imperative*, trans. Olive Wyon (Philadelphia: Westminster Press, 1947), p. 134.

3. Cf. Jean-Paul Sartre, *Existentialism and Humanism*, trans. Philip Mairet (London: Methuen, 1950).

4. Joseph Fletcher, *Situation Ethics: The New Morality* (Philadelphia: Westminster Press, 1966), p. 42.

5. *Ibid.*, p. 26.
6. *Ibid.*, p. 30.
7. *Ibid.*, p. 31.
8. *Ibid.*, p. 33. The quotation is from Dietrich Bonhoeffer, *Ethics*, trans. Neville Horton Smith (New York: Macmillan, 1955), p. 185.
9. Fletcher, *op. cit.*, p. 60.
10. *Ibid.*, p. 62.
11. *Ibid.*, p. 14.
12. *Ibid.*, p. 63.
13. These hyphenated phrases might suggest a Heideggerian approach unless I point out that other authors are specifically in mind here. More pertinent, owing to their development of the personal and incarnational dimensions of this matter, are Michael Polanyi's *Personal Knowledge* (Chicago: The University of Chicago Press, 1958) and Maurice Merleau-Ponty's *Phenomenology of Perception*, trans. C. Smith (New York: Humanities Press, 1962).
14. Fletcher, *op. cit.*, p. 59.
15. *Ibid.*, p. 60.
16. *Ibid.*, p. 52.
17. G. F. Woods, "The Grounds of Christian Moral Judgments," *Soundings*, ed. A. R. Vidler (New York: Cambridge University Press, 1962), p. 207.
18. Fletcher, *op. cit.*, p. 14.
19. *Ibid.*, p. 65.
20. It is, one thinks, of more than passing interest and somewhat ironic that in an earlier book Fletcher wrote passionately and persuasively of the obligation always to tell the truth; cf. Joseph Fletcher, *Morals and Medicine* (Princeton: Princeton University Press, 1954), chap. 2.
21. Fletcher, *Situation Ethics*, p. 75.
22. Cf. Hans Jonas, *The Gnostic Religion* (2d ed. rev.; Boston: Beacon Press, 1963), pp. 42-47 and especially pp. 320 ff., which demonstrates the excarnate character of these approaches.
23. Günther Bornkamm, *Jesus of Nazareth*, trans. Irene and Fraser McLuskey with James M. Robinson (New York: Harper & Bros., 1960), p. 116.
24. Daniel Day Williams, *God's Grace and Man's Hope* (New York: Harper & Bros., 1949), p. 78.
25. John Dourley, "Human Life—The Conciliar Teaching," *The Ecumenist*, IV (July-August, 1966), 80 f.

CHAPTER 6

1. The reader may be interested in viewing the new situational morality in the light of a historical analysis of the science of moral theology, for some of the criticisms of situational morality against traditional moral theology are not particularly new, nor has moral theology always maintained that monolithic unanimity of approach which situational morality seems to suspect. From earliest Christian times moral theology has evinced a certain tension between the more personalist approach and that juridical approach with which situational ethics charges it today. The objection that the new morality makes against the negative and minimizing tendency of moral theology is not especially new either. It has been made before and from within the science itself, by capable moral theologians, who actually grasped the complexity of principles and cross-principles that go into the formation of moral judgments. For a brief analysis, cf. my article "Situational Morality," *Thought,* XXXII (1957), 536-48.

CHAPTER 7

1. Cf. G. K. Chesterton, *Orthodoxy* (New York: Dodd, Mead & Co., 1959).
2. *Ibid.,* pp. 186 f.
3. Joseph Fletcher, *Situation Ethics: The New Morality* (Philadelphia: Westminster Press, 1966), p. 13.
4. *Ibid.,* p. 33.
5. Chesterton, *op. cit.,* p. 85.
6. Fletcher, *op. cit.,* p. 77.
7. *Ibid.,* p. 89.
8. *Ibid.,* p. 98.
9. *Ibid.,* p. 124. Cf. Alexander Miller, *The Renewal of Man,* ed. Reinhold Niebuhr (New York: Doubleday, 1955), pp. 99 f.
10. Fletcher, *op. cit.,* pp. 142 f.
11. *Ibid.,* p. 57.
12. Robert Fitch, "The Protestant Sickness," *Religion in Life,* XXXV, 4 (Autumn, 1966), 499.
13. Fletcher, *op. cit.,* p. 69.
14. *Ibid.,* p. 87.
15. *Ibid.,* p. 103.

16. *Ibid.*, p. 120.
17. *Ibid.*, p. 134.
18. Cf. William Temple, *Mens Creatrix* (New York: St. Martin's Press), p. 206, as quoted in Fletcher, *op. cit.*, p. 8.
19. John W. Gardner, *Self-Renewal: The Individual and the Innovative Society* (Harper Colophon Books; New York: Harper & Row, 1965), p. 39.

CHAPTER 8

1. Vernon L. Weiss, *The Christian Century*, LXXXIII, 50 (December 14, 1966), 1542.
2. Robert O. Johann, S.J., "Love and Justice," *Ethics and Society*, ed. R. T. DeGeorge (New York: Doubleday, 1966), pp. 33 f.
3. Francis Simons, "The Catholic Church and the New Morality," *Crosscurrents*, XVI, 4 (Fall, 1966), 429-45.
4. Bernard Häring, C.SS.R., *Toward a Christian Moral Theology* (South Bend, Ind.: University of Notre Dame Press, 1966), p. 206.
5. Cf. Rudolph Bultmann, *Jesus and the Word*, trans. Louise Pettibone Smith and Erminie Huntress Lantero (New York: Charles Scribner's Sons, 1958), p. 84.
6. Joseph Sittler, *The Structure of Christian Ethics* (Baton Rouge: Louisiana State University Press, 1958), chap. 1.
7. John A. T. Robinson, *Honest to God* (Philadelphia: Westminster Press, 1963), p. 115.
8. Cf. William Frankena, "Love and Principle in Christian Ethics," in A. Plantinga, *Faith and Philosophy* (Grand Rapids, Mich.: Eerdmans, 1954), pp. 207 f.
9. Paul Ramsey, *War and the Christian Conscience* (Durham, N.C.: Duke University Press, 1961). Cf. also his exchange with John C. Bennett in *America*, CXIV (1966), 119-40.
10. H. Richard Niebuhr, *The Purpose of the Church and Its Ministry* (New York: Harper & Bros., 1956), pp. 31-39.
11. James M. Gustafson, "Context Versus Principles: A Misplaced Debate in Christian Ethics," *Harvard Theological Review*, LVIII, 2 (April, 1965), 171 ff.
12. Cf. James A. Pike, *A Time for Christian Candor* (New York: Harper & Row 1964), especially pp. 10 f. and 120 f.; and Leslie

Dewart, *The Future of Belief* (New York: Herder & Herder, 1966), *passim*.
13. John G. Milhaven, S.J., *Theological Studies*, XXVII (1966), 483 ff.
14. W. O. Cross, "The Moral Revolution: An Analysis, Critique, and Appreciation," *Anglican Theological Review*, XVIII, 4 (1966), 356-79.